*Backgrounds
to Medieval
English
Literature*

D1306912

A Random House Study in Language and Literature

Backgrounds *to* Medieval English Literature

ROBERT W. ACKERMAN

Stanford University

RANDOM HOUSE   New York

9 8 7 6 5

© Copyright, 1966, by Random House, Inc.

All rights reserved under International and Pan-American
Copyright Conventions. Published in New York by Random
House, Inc. and simultaneously in Toronto, Canada, by
Random House of Canada Limited
Library of Congress Catalog Card Number: 66-26070
Manufactured in the United States of America by
H. Wolff Book Manufacturing Co., Inc., New York.

to RICHARD FOSTER JONES

Foreword

My aim in this book is to help the reader "naturalize" himself in the Middle Ages, to use C. S. Lewis's expression, so
that he may better understand and appreciate the eight
centuries of English literature bounded by the composition
of *Beowulf* and Caxton's edition of Malory's *Le Morte
Darthur*. I hope that this purpose is consistently reflected
in the organization and selection of material set forth here.

A "backgrounds" book or "introduction to literature"
intended for the student and also the general reader inevitably involves much quotation and suggestions for additional reading. The policies on such matters followed here
call for a short explanation. Passages from Old and Middle
English literature are generally quoted in the original language, especially in Chapter III, which deals with linguistic
backgrounds. For these, either a full translation or glossarial
notes are supplied. The translations, unless otherwise noted,
are mine. For easier reference by students, a number of
literary passages are cited from widely used textbooks or
anthologies, such as *Bright's Anglo-Saxon Reader* and Fernand Mossé's *Handbook of Middle English*, as indicated in
the footnotes. The Selective Bibliography, Part A, at the
end of the book, directs the student to the standard, critical
editions of the works of literature quoted or alluded to
throughout.

Following the Introduction, each of the five chapters,
and the Appendix is a list of Further Readings designed

to aid those who become interested in pursuing special topics. These lists, and also the citations in the footnotes, are supplemented by the books and articles making up Part B of the Selective Bibliography. The student may most efficiently improve on the bibliographical assistance offered here by turning to two readily available publications of recent date. The first of these—David A. Zesmer and Stanley B. Greenfield, *Guide to English Literature from Beowulf Through Chaucer and Medieval Drama*, College Outline Series, 1961—combines its well-annotated bibliographies with good historical sketches. On a more advanced level is *The Medieval Literature of Western Europe: A Review of Research, Mainly 1930–1960*, edited by John Hurt Fisher, New York: New York University Press, 1966. This book, the pre-publication text of which was made available to me, is a compilation of surveys of twentieth-century scholarship devoted to each of the important literatures of Western Europe in the Middle Ages: Latin, Celtic, Germanic (including Old Norse), Old French, other Romance languages, and English. Of prime interest to users of the present book, of course, are the two chapters on Old and Middle English literature by George K. Anderson and Robert W. Ackerman, respectively.

As must every teacher, I feel deeply indebted to my students over the years for no small number of the insights included here. Colleagues and friends have been generous in sharing their learning or in reading and criticizing the whole or parts of the manuscript, thus saving me from many errors. In particular, I wish to thank Professor Herbert Dean Meritt and the late Professor Francis R. Johnson, both of Stanford University, Professor Fred C. Robinson of Cornell University, and Professor Günter Freudenberg of the Pädagogische Hochschule, Osnabrück. To my wife's sound literary judgment and sophistication, to say nothing of her hard work, I owe more than I can say.

R. W. A.

Contents

FIGURES

Introduction

The writings surviving to us from the early centuries of English literary history—the eighth through the fifteenth centuries—are surprisingly numerous, especially in view of the fact that the invention of printing did not come until the very end of the Middle Ages. This literature inevitably reflects in many ways the momentous cultural changes that swept medieval England. The age beginning, say, with the composition of *Beowulf* in approximately 725 and continuing to 1474, when Caxton, still on the Continent, published the first book ever printed in English, was marked by political and social upheavals, including two periods of foreign domination, which, with respect to cultural significance, may not easily be matched in world history. The present book attempts to survey a number of these vicissitudes in the hope of promoting a sounder understanding and appreciation of English medieval literature. Much attention is given here to the characterization of medieval Christianity, for in nearly every aspect of life in this age religion was of sovereign importance.

Within the seven- or eight-century time span known as the Middle Ages in England, literary historians conventionally draw a heavy line between the writings preceding the Norman Conquest of 1066, the Old English or Anglo-Saxon period, and those dating from after the Conquest through the fifteenth century, the Middle English period. Here, however, the literary culture of the Old and Middle

English periods is treated as a continuum so far as possible, largely because the post-Conquest literature is all too likely to be half understood or even badly misconstrued when studied apart from the earlier literature. For example, the fluent prose employed in *Ancrene Riwle,* or "Rule of Ancresses," written in about 1200, and in other devotional and mystical works in Middle English quite plainly preserves the native tradition of homiletic prose going back into Old English times. To remain ignorant of this continuity invites a misunderstanding of the achievement and perhaps of the basic English qualities of the later writers.

Taken by themselves, pre-Conquest writings represent a small proportion of the total literary output of the period. We have, in fact, only about 30,000 lines of Old English poetry and fewer than 1,000 pages of prose of all kinds, including legal documents and other non-literary material. A small shelf, then, could accommodate all the Old English we possess, a considerable contrast to the great bulk of the Middle English corpus. We must recall, however, that both the Old and the Middle English writings remaining to us are chance survivors of an indefinitely larger production. On the basis of casual clues, such as Chaucer's allusion to "Wade's boat," it has been conjectured that, so far as the earlier period is concerned, we have lost much heroic poetry and narrative verse and prose, whereas little of importance in religious and didactic prose has vanished altogether. Of works in Middle English, relatively few romances or religious treatises have disappeared, but it is thought that heavy losses have occurred in the shorter narrative forms, such as the fabliaux and beast fables, and also in lyric poetry and drama. Very likely, some of the "lost literature" to which more or less clear references exist was never written down at all but was known solely by word of mouth. Another factor that must figure in our reconstruction of the literary scene is a recognition that Anglo-Latin and Anglo-French writings—that is, works written in Latin and French by English authors—are often significant. Again, no small part of the prose in Old English was translated from Latin, and in Middle English times many romances and religious works were taken directly from the French. Throughout the post-Conquest period, in fact, English competed from a socially inferior position with both Latin and French, emerging as undisputed victor no earlier than the fourteenth century.

Of obvious importance to the reader is an understanding of shifts in the system of values informing medieval literature. The abandonment or compromising of the pagan Germanic ethos, with its emphasis on the heroic ideal, and the concurrent acceptance of Christian teachings may be observed in even the earlier Old English poetry, *Beowulf* included. Echoes of the old fatalism and battle lust continue to be heard, but they are at length subdued by the growing trend toward Christian didacticism. In itself, of course, an instructional or consciously edifying purpose need not limit the achievement of a good poet, as may be illustrated by the beautiful ninth-century address of the Cross to the dreamer, known as *The Dream of the Rood*. After England was brought more fully into the European community by the Conquest of 1066, the didactic note became even stronger. Virtually all serious writing was concerned in some way with inculcating the Christian virtues or lauding the divine symmetry of the Christian world view. The moralists of the day bitterly denounced minstrels for their immoral songs and performances, with special reference to the knightly romance, a form which English poets began to practice in the thirteenth century in imitation of the French. Possibly clerical disapproval of frivolous tales of "wild adventure in love and chivalry," to quote Dr. Samuel Johnson, played a part in the evolution of the Christianized romance, of which the greatest examples are the magnificent epic of the Holy Grail and *Sir Gawain and the Green Knight*.

Some insight into the changes that overtook the English language in medieval times is even more essential to intelligent reading. Responding to long and intimate contact with Old Norse and Norman French, that variety of

French spoken by the Norman invaders, the language of
the Anglo-Saxons evolved by the thirteenth century into
something recognizably close to Modern English in structure and vocabulary. These linguistic developments, and
especially the naturalization of words taken from Latin,
Norse, and French, provide the clearest evidence we have
of the penetration of Anglo-Saxon civilization by foreigners.
Related to such considerations is the impact on Old English
literary forms and conventions of Latin and French poetry.
In particular, the alliterative measure, used in Old English
as in all other Germanic literatures, came ultimately to be
supplanted by metrical, rimed verse in imitation of Latin
and Old French practices. Perhaps rime would have developed natively without benefit of foreign models. At least,
we find experiments in this direction by the poet Cynewulf
in the ninth century. On the other hand, Layamon, when
writing his *Brut* in about 1200, was quite likely inspired to
enrich his alliterative lines with occasional rime by the
example set by Wace, whose French poem he was translating.

Finally, the modern reader generally needs to expand
and liberalize his notion of literature when approaching
the Middle Ages. He must be prepared to admit not only
the genres normally classified as *belles lettres* but also the
works of annalists and clerics bent, it may seem to him,
largely on instruction and exhortation. He will find in Middle English many works like *Cursor Mundi*, or "Over-
Runner of the World," poetic in form but didactic in conception and removed from what he usually regards as
imaginative appeal. For the man of the Middle Ages, as
will be explained in later chapters, historical and scientific
truth merged into moral and religious truth. It was because
human involvement was felt so strongly in everything that
happened and everything that existed that history and
science or pseudo-science were commonly accorded, along
with pure fiction, what may be called a literary treatment.
Something of a parallel may be seen in the rather ecstatic
tone and the invocation to Venus in Lucretius's Latin

classic, *On the Nature of Things*, which sets forth the atomic theory of matter. A "literary treatment" does not necessarily imply the use of verse rather than prose, although this was generally true throughout most of the Middle English period. Middle English prose was strangely late in marking out what came to be its proper sphere, and poetry, or at least rimed couplets, continued as the standard vehicle for strictly practical as well as literary purposes. Not until the fifteenth century, in fact, was prose fully accepted in narrative, as in Malory's *Le Morte Darthur*.

There are, of course, several works in Old and Middle English to all or to parts of which a present-day reader will respond favorably even if he is totally devoid of "background" information of the sort to be presented here. Portions at least of *Beowulf* and Chaucer's *General Prologue* certainly fall in this category. But the temper of the twentieth century probably inhibits spontaneous approval of counsels to perfection, discourses on God's Providence, and perhaps of leisurely literary forms, such as dream-vision allegories. Because of its moral and theological orientation, a very large body of literature, including that which was closest to the heart and mind of the Middle Ages, is likely to prove alien and difficult to one who has not sought to acclimate himself in the age. Without such an effort, Old English sermons will seem to him little more than dreary laments about moral lapses and social evils. Moreover, he may value for the wrong reasons even that which does appeal to him. That is, he may tend to prize Chaucer only for his worldly wisdom and "modern" sense of humor and also what he takes, in profound error, to be modern skepticism. He will miss entirely or seriously misapprehend the spiritual overtones in *Sir Gawain and the Green Knight*. To him, *Piers Plowman* will be an incoherent series of dialogues among personifications which is readable only because one unexpectedly and infrequently encounters vivid sketches of fourteenth-century life, as in the often-quoted "Confession of the Seven Deadly Sins."

In this book, selected aspects of cultural history are

treated in the following order: social and religious backgrounds of the Old English and Middle English periods
respectively, the English language, popular Christian doctrine, and the world view of the Middle Ages. In addition,
a brief survey of various critical approaches to medieval
literature is included as an appendix. An effort has been
made to restrict the discussion of each topic to that which
is germane to the understanding of literature, and frequent
allusions are made to the most widely read works, particularly *Beowulf* and the works of Chaucer, by way of illustrating the cogency of the information. At the end of each
chapter stands a short list of readings for further study.

The present work, it may be seen, differs from other
"background" books and "companions" to literature. That
is, it is broader in scope, chronologically speaking, than
Basil Willey's *The Seventeenth-Century Background*, which
concentrates on the period from Francis Bacon to John
Locke and is oriented particularly to a discussion of Milton's
Paradise Lost. And, in contrast to C. S. Lewis's recent *The
Discarded Image* and E. M. W. Tillyard's *The Elizabethan
World Picture*, both valuable treatments of cosmological
ideas and directly related concepts, the present work seeks
to reconstruct not only the world view of the Middle Ages
but several other phases of cultural and intellectual history
as well. It is also more intimately concerned with English
literature than Christopher Dawson's *Medieval Essays*, a
valuable introduction to the Christian culture, the theology,
and the science of the Middle Ages.

To assume that this survey will dispel all misappre-
hensions and bring about a happy consensus in the understanding and evaluation of early English literature would
be somewhat akin to the immodest and patronizing opti-
mism voiced by Robert Mannyng of Brunne in *Handlyng
Synne* (1303), a delightful collection of tales illustrating
vices and virtues:

> For lewde men y vndyr-toke
> On englyssh tunge to make þys boke.

For many ben of swyche manere,
þat talys and rymys wyl bleþly here;
Yn gamys, & festys, & at þe ale,
Loue men to lestene troteuale:
þat may falle ofte to vylanye,
To dedly synne, or oþer folye;
For swyche men haue y made þis ryme
þat þey may weyl dyspende here tyme,
And þere-yn sumwhat for to here,
To leue all swyche foul manere.*

For ignorant (lewd) men I undertook
To write this book in the English tongue.
For many are of such a nature,
That they will gladly listen to tales and rimes;
At games, at feasts, and at ale,
Men love to listen to idle talk:
And this may often lead to villainous acts,
To deadly sin, or to some other folly;
For such men have I written this rime
In order that they will spend their time well,
And learn something from it,
That will cause them to leave off their foul way of life.

FURTHER READINGS

Bennett, H. S., "Medieval Literature and the Modern Reader," *Essays and Studies by Members of the English Association,* XXXI (1946), 7–18.
[The need for inquiring into the ideas and conventions of the age when studying medieval literature is amply illustrated here.]

Dawson, Christopher, *Medieval Essays,* New York: Sheed and Ward, 1954.

Dean, Ruth J., "What Is Anglo-Norman?" *Annuale Mediaevale,* VI (1965), 29–46.

* Robert Mannyng of Brunne, *Handlyng Synne,* Frederick J. Furnivall, ed., Early English Text Society, CXIX, CXXIII (1901, 1903), ll. 43–54.

Lewis, C. S., *The Discarded Image: An Introduction to Medieval and Renaissance Literature*, Cambridge, Eng.: University Press, 1964.
[The formation of the medieval world view out of numerous ideas stemming from late classical times is brilliantly treated here.]

Tillyard, E. M. W., *The Elizabethan World Picture*, London: Chatto and Windus, 1958.

Wilson, R. M., *The Lost Literature of Medieval England*, London: Methuen, 1952.

Backgrounds
to
Medieval

English

Literature

I. Social and Religious Backgrounds: Old English Period

To survey systematically the socio-political, intellectual, and religious context of early English literature is obviously out of the question here. Yet, as indicated in the Introduction, we need urgently to acquire some notion of the changing values or ideals of the age, an inquiry which involves at least a broad understanding of medieval society, with special reference to education and literacy and the religiously dominated intellectual life as well. Of similar importance is a grasp of the basic nature of the English language and of the ways in which it changed in response to various influences. In the present chapter on Old English backgrounds and in those that follow, political events and dates are mentioned only when they have literary or linguistic significance or serve to establish a chronological framework for the presentation of aspects of cultural history.

The English literature preserved to us seems to begin in the seventh or eighth century, even though the traditions it embodies go back to the settlement age, the fifth and sixth centuries, and possibly to the tribal life of the Anglian, Saxon, and Jutish peoples before they left the Continent.

The student must remember that the few manuscripts containing Old English literature were written down after the time of composition and sometimes long after. To approximate roughly the composition dates of Old English writings is a complex and uncertain task because of the likelihood that they were subjected to updating and other kinds of modification in the process of transmission. The problem of deciding how much a given work owes to a series of oral composers and how much to later literary redactors is equally difficult. Historical scholars, then, when assigning a date can do little more than to indicate the half-century during which the author presumably flourished. Since the development of written English had to await the assimilation of the Latin culture brought to England by missionaries in 597, it is not surprising that the earliest literature of record dates from the seventh century.

The poem *Widsith*[1] furnishes an example of the problems involved. This 143-line poem occurring only in the Exeter Book, a manuscript of the late tenth century, is considered to have been composed in the late seventh century although certain of its thulas, or mnemonic catalogues of kings and tribes, may go back three hundred years further. Although there are differences of opinion, scholars generally assign *Beowulf*, the *Finnsburg* epic, of which only fragments survive, *Deor's Lament*, *The Wanderer*, and *The Seafarer* to the early part of the "classical age" (eighth and early ninth century), whereas the poems of Cynewulf, such as *Juliana*, *Christ*, and *Elene*, are of a somewhat later origin. *Waldere*, another epic fragment, is probably early, and *The Dream of the Rood*, known to us in the Vercelli Manuscript of perhaps 1000 A.D., is quite likely a reworking of an earlier poem. That is, lines from what may well be an antecedent version are inscribed on the Ruthwell monumental cross in Dumfriesshire, Scotland, said to have been carved in the eighth century. The historical poems *Brunanburh* and *Maldon* were written in commemoration of battles taking place in 937 and 991 respectively. *Brunanburh* is preserved under the appropriate date in the *Saxon Chroni-*

cle, along with a few other poems set down by annalists as part of tenth- and eleventh-century entries. Old English literary prose, a later development than poetry, did not emerge until the reign of King Alfred (849-899). In that period and later, the quality of the prose in a number of translations, prefaces, and homilies rises far above the bare requirements of communication. In fact, the prose of Alfred and his coadjutors was the starting point of the fine tradition of religious writing that continued throughout the Middle Ages.

A general awareness of Anglo-Saxon culture and its heritage is especially important to the reader of the Old English poets and prose writers. More specifically, many if not most of these works demand of modern readers at least modest enlightenment on such matters as the organization of society, the relations of lord to retainers, the function and status of the minstrel or *scop* (pronounced "shope"), the dim survivals of Germanic paganism, the hall culture of thane, earl, and alderman, and the penetration of Christian ethics and Christian learning.

At least as early as the seventh century, the Anglo-Saxons outgrew the tribal society which they had maintained in their continental homes. But the social forms and the culture that evolved were only slightly touched by the decayed Romano-Celtic civilization that the Germanic invaders displaced. It is said that the newcomers shunned the Roman structures still standing and that they even avoided old town sites. A poetic reflection of this superstitious attitude is to be found in *The Ruin,* preserved in the Exeter Book, although it is difficult to decide whether the crumbling towers and lichen-covered stonework mentioned there describe dilapidated buildings in Bath or the Roman wall in Northumbria. At the same time, the Anglo-Saxons made use of the astonishingly durable Roman highways stretching across the country, such as Watling Street, Ermine Street, and Foss Way. Also, the Christianity brought to Britain in the third century from Rome remained alive among the Britons who retreated into the "Celtic fringe"

—that is, Wales, Cornwall, Scotland, and Brittany. The Welsh Christians themselves made little effort to redeem the hated Saxons from their heathenism, but the later missionary activity by the Scots, especially the mission of St. Aidan in 635, resulted in the conversion of Northumbria. By this time, the Christianization of England south of the Humber River beginning with St. Augustine's advent in 597 was well under way.

A number of small Anglo-Saxon kingdoms came into being at an early date, the kingship in each being reserved to those families claiming descent from Germanic divinities, chiefly Woden. A series of consolidations resulted in seven different states of which Kent, Northumbria, Mercia, and Wessex were the most stable and important. Kent appears to have been especially influential during the reign of Æthelberht or Ethelbert (late sixth century), who received Augustine's mission and was himself converted. Northumbria, the border kingdom, was unified by Æthelfrith in the seventh century, and Æthelfrith's successor, Edwin, achieved some authority over the southern kingdoms besides beating back the Scots and Picts. The newly imported Christian culture soon produced in this region the scholar-bishop, Aldhelm, and at the monastery of St. Paul at Jarrow, the much greater scholar, St. Bede (673-735). The North may also claim Alcuin, who, after his schooling at York, became famous as the educational adviser in the court of Charlemagne. Northern culture continued to flourish even after the power of Northumbria succumbed to that of the Midland Kingdom of Mercia under the successors of Penda, one of the last important pagans.

Wessex on the Channel coast was a loose association of petty states until the late seventh century. A Wessex king, Cynegils, is recorded as having accepted Christianity in 635, and a later ruler, Ine, drew up a code of laws. It was under Ecgbert (d. 839), however, that Wessex first attained to hegemony over much of England, and although Wessex authority waned after 839, Ecgbert may be said to have laid the foundations of the strongly unified kingdom of Alfred. Alfred's magnificent achievement, along with his sponsorship of learning and religion, was his valorous and successful stand against the Danish invaders. The Danes mounted a number of isolated attacks on England between 835 and 865, but in the latter year a large army occupied East Anglia, came to control Northumbria, and penetrated into Wessex. Alfred was crowned in the midst of battle, and, as the annalists of the *Saxon Chronicle*[2] report, he had few breathing spells throughout his entire reign. The Peace of Wedmore, which in 879 he was able to force on his chief enemy, gave the king some relief, but the Vikings descended again in the early 890's, and the English were still beleaguered when Alfred died at the end of the century. One of the momentous administrative measures called forth by the desperate circumstances was the settlement of the Danes in the Danelaw, the northern and eastern section of England bounded by Watling Street, which runs northwest from London toward Chester. The Danes taking up land here maintained their old legal customs, although the English kings appointed their earls and bishops and imposed militia service on them. Christianity seems to have been accepted peacefully enough.

Largely because of the record of Alfred's zeal for reviving religion and literacy in his ravaged land, we know something about the cultural state of late ninth-century England. In the famous Preface to his translations from Pope Gregory's *Pastoral Care*, Alfred registers the almost complete disappearance of the Latin learning which had earlier flourished in his kingdom and which had attracted many foreigners. The churches filled with treasures and books whose destruction by the Danes the king laments[3] were largely monastic institutions, it seems.

It is true that Vikings settled in Ireland attacked and occupied parts of the West Midlands of England and York where they constituted a threat until a coalition of Northerners and Scots was defeated in 947 at an unidentified site called Brunanburh. It was this battle that inspired the fine historical poem inserted in the *Saxon Chronicle*. Generally speaking, however, after Alfred's time the Scandinavians caused no great trouble in England until the last years of the tenth century when Danes and Norwegians resumed the incursions leading ultimately to the short-lived but important Anglo-Danish state in the first half of the eleventh century. The tenth century was marked chiefly by the gradual assimilation of the Danelaw, the consolidation of all England as a nation, especially under Edward the Elder and his son Athelstan (901–940), the beginnings of the shire system, and the partial re-establishment of the monasteries. The reign of Edgar (959–975) saw considerable ecclesiastical advance, especially as the result of efforts by St. Dunstan, who became Archbishop of Canterbury in 960, and Oswald, Archbishop of York (d. 992), to establish monasteries on reformed principles and to revitalize the whole of the English Church.

The so-called Second Coming of the Danes beginning in the 980's is fittingly commemorated in literature by the poem *Maldon*, which depicts in the language of the ancient heroic tradition the defeat of Byrhtnoth, Alderman of Essex, by a body of Viking invaders in 991. The confusion of the following two or three decades was intense, but, for reasons ascribable to the ineptitude of King Æthelred Unræd, or the Redeless (d. 1016), Cnut the Dane was crowned king of England in 1016. Throughout his nineteen-year reign, this foreign king sought with uneven success to control three Scandinavian kingdoms while remaining for the most part in his conquered realm of England. Cnut ruled vigorously and conscientiously, promoting Christianity and issuing a great legal code to his English subjects. With Scandinavians in positions of highest authority, it is not surprising that the English tended at this time to borrow Norse words. Thus, following Danish practice, the English came to call great administrative officers by the title of *eorl* (Norse *jarl*) instead of *ealdormonn*.

In 1042, after the brief reigns of Harold Harefoot and Harthacnut, the Danish line failed and Edward the Confessor, son of Æthelred, was elected king. At this point,

Norman influence began to make itself felt strongly in the English court, and it continued despite the nationalistic movement led by Godwine, Earl of Wessex, and his sons. One of these sons, Harold, was placed on the English throne in January 1066, for the final brief act of Anglo-Saxon history. After crushing a Norwegian invasion of Yorkshire led by the King of Norway, Harold marched to the south and was defeated and slain by William of Normandy at Hastings.

Anglo-Saxons experienced few intervals of peace and serenity. Especially in view of long series of internecine wars and of Scandinavian invasions, the political and social instability of the age is scarcely surprising. The Angles, Saxons, and Jutes of the fifth-century settlements were headed by their petty kings and a class of nobles made up of the kings' companions or members of their war bands. Although there were slaves enjoying little legal protection throughout Anglo-Saxon history, as we know from a famous sermon by Bishop Wulfstan in the early eleventh century, the mass of men were free farmers, or churls, who held their lands directly from their kings. As early law codes indicate, the slayer of a churl was obliged to pay a heavy fine called *wergeld* to the kinsmen of the victim besides a smaller fine to the king. For his parcel of farm land, called a "hide," which varied in size from one part of England to another, the free farmer paid a food tax called *feorm* (Modern English "farm") to the king, and he was also bound to serve in the militia or *fyrd* of his district in time of war. Although open-field agricultural methods prevailed in a great part of England, the acreage held by an individual was understood to be his personal property rather than a share of common ownership. In the reign of William the Conqueror the Anglo-Saxon social organization came to be modified by the introduction of Norman feudalism. Isolated farms were to be found, but a large proportion of the farmers lived in tiny villages. The village, in fact, was the standard unit of rural organization.

Throughout the period, a steady drift of the free peasantry toward some form of servitude is apparent. **Of the** forces which combined to bring about what has been called Anglo-Saxon feudalism, the most important stemmed from the perils and the heavy burdens of warfare and invasion borne by the rural inhabitants. The consolidation of small kingdoms into larger ones, the practice of kings of assigning to thanes and bishops authority over large tracts of land, and the emulation of this practice by the chief lords in rewarding their own retainers created the decentralization typical of feudalism. At the same time, farmers, driven to the wall by the endemic invasions and by assessments needed for the enormous bribes paid to faithless Danish marauders, began to put themselves under the military protection of local magnates, binding themselves to servitude on the lord's demesne. By the ceremony of homage, the churl turned over his land to the lord, swearing to be his man, in return for protection. In the mid-tenth century, it appears that local lords had been given the right to set up manorial courts and to dispense justice to their tenants.

Organizational patterns and legal customs differed somewhat from one part of the country to another, but toward the end of the Anglo-Saxon era certain social classes are distinguishable. Besides the territorial magnates, such as the earls who ruled the shires, there was a superior class of peasants bound to their lord by certain occasional services, such as reaping or mowing on the demesne, but who were regarded as free men. Below this group was the far greater category of *geburas* or villeins who carried a very heavy burden of rents and services in return for undisturbed hereditary possession of their land, which typically amounted to a quarter-hide, or about thirty acres.

Relatively early in Anglo-Saxon times, the Church came to exert telling influence, spiritual, intellectual, and even political. But, antecedent to the full Christianization of the island, the heathen beliefs and practices of the Germanic settlers remained an active force, as is indicated both in Latin and Old English writings. That heathenism persisted well into and beyond the seventh century is amply attested by historians such as Bede and the writers of the *Saxon Chronicle*. Bede, in one of his works, etymologizes the Old English names of the months, tracing them to the names of deities of the Germanic pantheon. This he would scarcely have done had not some lingering knowledge of the old gods been alive in his day. The third and fourth months, for example, were called after Hretha and Eostre (Easter), and others had names taken from seasonal sacrifices. A number of geographical names yield to similar explanations: Thanet is said to be Thunor's field; Wednesfield, Woden's field; and Grimsdyke, Grim's dike, Grim being a by-name for Woden. In a letter written in about 797, Alcuin makes very clear that old pagan songs were still popular even among Christian priests:

> Let the words of God be read at priestly banquets. There it is fitting to listen to a reader, not to a harper; to the discourses of the Fathers, not to the songs of the heathen. What concord hath Ingeld with Christ? The house is too narrow to hold both.[4]

A somewhat analagous mixture of heathen lore and allusions to Christ appears in some of the remedies for physical ailments prescribed in the tenth-century *Leechdoms* and also in the Old English *Charms*.

In the course of his remarkable *Ecclesiastical History of the English People*, Bede, like the shadowy chronicler Gildas, has much to say about the conversion of the Anglo-Saxons. Most famous among these accounts is his story of Paulinus's mission to King Edwin of Northumbria in about 625. The principal spokesman in the tale is Edwin's chief priest, Coifi, or Cefi, who was moved to embrace Christianity himself and to advise his master to do likewise by two considerations: first, that he had never received satisfactory reward from the heathen gods for his faithful service; and second, that the new religion, unlike the old, offers teachings about what precedes and what follows man's brief span of life on earth. The second point is expounded in a beautiful parable spoken by a thane:

O king, the present life of man on earth seems to me, in comparison with the time of which we are ignorant, as if you were sitting at a feast with your chief men and thanes in the winter time, and a fire were kindled in the midst and the hall warmed, while everywhere outside there were raging whirlwinds of wintry rain and snow; and as if then there came a stray sparrow, and swiftly flew through the house, entering at one door and passing out through another. As long as he is inside, he is not buffeted by the winter's storm; but in the twinkling of an eye the lull for him is over, and he speeds from winter back to winter again, and is gone from your sight. So this life of man appeareth for a little time; but what cometh after, or what went before, we know not.[5]

In continuing his story, Bede describes Coifi's symbolic act of arming himself, and mounting a stallion, both acts forbidden to a pagan priest, and casting a spear into a nearby heathen place of worship. Temples or fanes where some sort of rites were celebrated are also accorded a bare mention in *Beowulf*, for the poet speaks of structures where the Danes prayed for help against Grendel (*æt hærgtrafum*, l. 175). In neither of these works nor in any other writings of the period is there anything approaching a satisfactory account of the old heathen beliefs and practices. Lacking altogether are Old English creation stories, descriptions of the cosmology, and myths of the divinities, such as exist in Old Norse. To assume that the Anglo-Saxons entertained originally the same set of religious concepts as did their North Germanic cousins is obviously unsafe. Our knowledge of Anglo-Saxon heathenism, then, remains vague, although it is apparent from history that the old religion, stubbornly resurgent as it was from time to time, was far too primitive and undeveloped to stand as a real rival to Christianity and that its priesthood was never especially influential.

On the other hand, Germanic peoples idealized almost

to the point of religious veneration the man who displayed reckless courage and prowess in battle or stoically endured great hardships, such as those of the sailor. Fundamental to the stories of Beowulf and others is the exaltation of extreme physical bravery. Even though the insensate, "berserker" rage of the Old Norse fighter is not found explicitly in Old English writings, to take grim joy in the dangerous life was clearly viewed as a high virtue. Like the superman of German epics, the Anglo-Saxon hero seems to be motivated by a longing for widespread renown. *Dom biŏ selast,* or "fame is best," is a common formulation of this desire, and the itinerant minstrels were relied on both to compose and to recite everywhere appropriate songs in honor of worthy men. In the heroic tales, the warrior normally fights or submits himself to other dangers out of a deep sense of loyalty—loyalty to his leader or lord, to his kindred, or to members of his *comitatus* or war band, especially to men to whom he is bound by an oath of blood brotherhood. Sometimes he is presented at a crucial point with an agonizing conflict of moral obligations. In *Waldere,* Hagen must decide whether his sworn loyalty to his chief Gunther lays on him a heavier obligation than his oath of brotherhood to Waldere, Gunther's adversary. In *Finnsburg,* Hengest's conflict is between the duty of exacting vengeance for the slaying of his late lord, Hnæf, and the terms of his peace treaty with Finn. Unlike the Greek dramatists, Anglo-Saxon poets were not much inclined to muse about the ultimate justice or correctness of the hero's choice in his dilemma; rather, they were interested in inviting admiration for his unflinching steadfastness in facing down the often bleak consequences of his course of action, whatever it was. The author of the late tenth-century historical poem *Maldon* expresses the heroic ethos as follows:

> Mind will be harder,   heart the keener,
> Courage the greater,   as our strength lessens.[6]

The old heathen concept of fate—*wyrd* in Old English —is a basic component of the heroic ideal. *Wyrd,* often on the lips of Anglo-Saxon poets, is generally no more than blind, irresponsible destiny. When Beowulf tells Hrothgar that, should he meet his death in conflict with Grendel, his heirloom byrnie is to be sent to Hygelac, he adds rather sententiously:

Fate always tends   whither she wishes.[7]

Behind a later passage, however, lurks an indistinct hint that superhuman valor may somehow earn a reversal of an earlier decision of fate:

                    Wyrd often spares
    An undoomed earl   if his courage holds out.[8]

Although in an early eighth-century glossary, *wyrd* is once equated with Latin *parcae*, or the goddesses of fate, the Anglo-Saxons were not interested in deifying destinal forces, if the surviving literature provides a reliable clue. Just as they felt no need to support their exaltation of physical courage and fortitude by allusions to Valhalla, the heaven of heroes, they were apparently oblivious to such fanciful personifications as the three Norns who people the later Scandinavian mythology.

The fifth-century Germanic invaders brought into England ways of life untouched by Roman civilization; indeed, they were regarded as barbarians by the Romans. Gildas, writing presumably in the sixth century, says that "they were hateful to God and man," and yet the Angles, Saxons, and Jutes were by no means primitive tribesmen. Many of them were seafarers, fishermen, and hunters, but they had also developed farming methods. Although they remained essentially illiterate until Roman missionaries brought the Latin language and alphabet into the island at the end of the sixth century, they had made the acquaintance through other Germanic peoples of runes and used them for inscriptions. They were accomplished artisans in metals and other materials, decorating their iron swords richly and fashioning distinctive jewelry and many kinds of art objects. They continued to practice these arts in England and apparently learned new techniques and designs from the Romanized Celts they had conquered. Their legal customs, which they finally committed to writing in the seventh century, represented a long and carefully maintained tradition of a fairly orderly society.

Although churls and slaves lived in relatively primitive huts in squalid villages, as was true of the rural populace throughout the Middle Ages and later, the hall culture of the Anglo-Saxons had a brilliance and luxury which we are only now beginning to appreciate. The most startling evidence to this effect was discovered in 1939, when a great barrow containing a ship laden with burial furniture was opened at Sutton Hoo, Suffolk. Since no corpse seems ever to have been deposited in the ship, it is surmised that we have here a cenotaph or memorial to a ruler who lived in East Anglia in the middle or latter part of the seventh century. Uncannily close parallels have been noted between this remarkable ship-cenotaph and two passages in *Beowulf* describing respectively the ship-passing of Scyld Scefing and, at the end of the poem, the interment of the firedragon's hoard. In fact, a reading of these passages from *Beowulf* (ll. 26 ff. and ll. 3156 ff.) persuaded a coroner's jury in 1939 that the original intention at Sutton Hoo had been a burial which should remain undisturbed and, therefore, that the treasure was to be considered the property of the landowner rather than of the crown. The person memorialized at Sutton Hoo is unknown, but several different East Anglian kings have been proposed as candidates—Rældwald, who died in the first years of the seventh century and who, because of his early date, is now generally ruled out of competition, and Æthelhere and Æthelwald, both of whom died well after 650. Although it has been assumed that the king honored according to an ancient heathen custom must himself have been heathen, the pair of silver spoons thought by some to be "baptismal spoons" has led certain authorities to identify him with the Christian Æthelwald instead of the possibly pagan Æthelhere.

Apart from the set of silver bowls marked with a cross

and possibly the spoons, the artifacts deposited in the great eighty-foot rowing ship are in keeping with pagan custom. Included are armor; a helmet with boar's head decorations; drinking horns, of which two are made from the giant horns (six-quart capacity) of the now extinct aurochs; a purse of cloisonné work containing Merovingian coins; symbols of high rank, such as an iron standard and a carved ceremonial whetstone; various pieces of intricately wrought jewelry; and the remains of a small, six-stringed harp. All these items, including the great rowing ship, are of intense archaeological interest; some of them are the only examples of their kind known to be extant, and the fragments of the harp are sufficiently numerous to enable experts to reconstruct the original instrument. With the Sutton Hoo treasures now in the British Museum in mind, the reader of Old English heroic poetry can supplement with authentic details the literary accounts of banquets and other ceremonial occasions in the king's hall. He can visualize the gifts exchanged by king and thane, the great meadhorn borne by the gracious queen as she passes from one noble guest to the next, and the *scop* standing before the high seat and singing to the accompaniment of his harp. It is also possible to bring into sharper focus the appearance and actions of warriors engaging in close combat or sweeping across the water in their ring-prowed ships. In general, the Sutton Hoo trove materially increases our respect for the splendor and sophistication of Anglo-Saxon courtly society.

Professor Wrenn believes that Sutton Hoo, with its mixture of pagan and Christian artifacts, provides a kind of analogue to seventh-century Anglo-Saxon society in which Woden and Christ were in confrontation.[9] Not all scholars are in agreement on this matter, but the fact remains that the work of Christianizing England and of founding a unified national church was not finished until about the middle of the eighth century. By that time, the Christian Scots, who had made great contributions to the proselytizing of the North, had reluctantly recognized the supremacy of the Roman Church at the Synod of Whitby, 664, and the old heathenism had been largely assimilated. The century and a half of missionary work, it is true, saw many reversals and frustrations. Wholesale conversions were sometimes followed by wholesale backsliding. Also, by reason of Pope Gregory's tolerant policies, no ruthless effort was made to stamp out all heathen customs. In general, heathen temples were destroyed, but there is a possibility that one or two were purged and turned into churches; moreover, certain old rites and sacrifices were converted into Christian feasts. In this way arose Whitsun and Church-ales, Yule-tide customs, and the like. Other vestiges of heathenism which survived are represented in folk superstitions, such as the Old English *Charms* and the magical remedies in *Leechdoms*, already mentioned.

From early times, the work begun by St. Augustine of Canterbury was carried out by monks, many of whom later became missionary bishops. The missionaries sent out by the Scots were also monks of the Celtic type who tended first to establish monasteries, such as Aidan's monastery at Lindisfarne, and then to fan out from those centers on preaching tours. Some "minsters" or churches containing "colleges" of clergy were established for the sake of administering to the spiritual needs of large areas within the dioceses, but the system of parishes or village churches was not complete even by the time of the Danish invasions.

St. Augustine received the pall of archbishop at the start of his mission, and his immediate successors sought to decentralize their endeavors by creating some fourteen dioceses conforming more or less to the geographical distribution of the different Germanic peoples in England. Thus, the See of Rochester was established for the West Kentish people in about 604, the year of Augustine's death, and that of London for the East Saxons in the same year. The bishopric of York served the Northumbrians from 625, not becoming an archbishopric until 735. Especially during the terrible Danish invasions of the ninth century, the original diocesan boundaries were considerably altered. Cathedral churches seem initially to have been served by regular clergy—that is, by monks—but these communities, along with all religious houses, were particularly tempting to the marauders, with the result that many monks were slain and their buildings and libraries destroyed. This blow to culture and religion in Anglo-Saxon England was devastating, as King Alfred clearly recognized at the time. It is true that the later Scandinavian invaders, those of the eleventh century, were nearly all Christians, but religious scruples did not prevent their sacking Canterbury in 1011 and martyring Archbishop Ælfheah (St. Elphege) the following year.

As a result of the spoliation of the religious houses in the ninth and tenth centuries, secular priests came to staff the cathedrals and larger churches in place of the monks, a situation deplored by many because of the poor reputation of the secular clergy for discipline and learning. St. Dunstan's reforms, mentioned above, led not only to the founding of a number of monasteries but also to the formation by the year 1000 of monastic chapters at such cathedrals as Canterbury and Sherborne. During the ensuing century, the strength of the monasteries increased, but the secular clergy may not be said to have improved greatly in quality. At the time of the great Domesday Survey in 1086, the population of England proper is estimated to have been 1,100,000 of which 98 per cent were rural inhabitants—that is, peasant villagers. Serving the population of England in the thousands of parishes were perhaps 4,000 beneficed priests. In addition there were 750 monks distributed among 35 monastic houses, and a few communities of nuns besides.[10]

During the four centuries immediately preceding the Conquest, the period of literary production, England was a Christian nation, despite the pockets of Danish heathenism that yielded slowly to conversion. The nearness of the Anglo-Saxons to their heathenism is most apparent in seventh- and eighth-century writings, but it also shows up sporadically and in oblique ways in later literature as well. The grim fatalism or melancholy of the elegiac poems is a pagan inheritance, it seems, although it was sometimes presented in a Christian guise by poets and redactors. Even

the Biblical paraphrases ascribed to Cædmon and the poetic saints' lives carry over the kennings and some of the
battle-lust of pre-Christian times. In explicitly Christian
poems offering, it would seem, little scope for such exulta-
tion, like Cynewulf's *Christ* and *The Dream of the Rood*,
the old idiom unexpectedly breaks through. That the memory of the heroic past and the ancient modes of expression
were kept green, probably in an active oral tradition, is
demonstrated by the composition of tenth-century poems
such as *Brunanburh* and *Maldon*.

The influence of Christianity and the Latin culture it
brought in its train is evident in nearly all Old English
literature, including heroic narratives dealing primarily with
Germanic legends and attitudes. For example, the belief
that the *Beowulf*-poet knew Virgil's *Aeneid* has been seriously argued. No one doubts that *Beowulf* contains many
Christian allusions, but a disparity of views prevails as to
the centrality of Christian ideas in the poem. The editor of
Beowulf, Friedrich Klaeber, has said that "we might even
feel inclined to recognize features of the Christian Savior in
the destroyer of hellish fiends." [11] More recently, other
scholars have held that *Beowulf* is an allegory of salvation
or at least of Christian charity. Rather than imputing to
the poet a basic Christian-didactic intention, most critics
interested in this aspect of the work remain content with
noting occasional evidence of the poet's knowledge of
Christian poetry, of the Christian concepts of grace and
election, and of the baptismal liturgy.[12]

Latin culture also had an immediate and obvious effect
on the writing of prose. Apart from purely matter-of-fact
records like deeds, the earliest prose written by Englishmen
was in Latin. Very likely, it would never have occurred to
Bede to write his *Ecclesiastical History of the English People* or any of his other historical or his scientific works in
English. Plainly responsible for the falling-off of Latin
prose and the rather sudden flourishing of English, under
Alfred and his circle, was the destruction of the monasteries
and the slaughter or dispersal of the learned men of the

kingdom. Paradoxically, the disappearance of the centers of learning and education may also be responsible for what seems to be the virtual drying-up of the stream of Anglo-Saxon poetry in the tenth and eleventh centuries. It has been suggested that the traditional poetry ceased to be written or appreciated in these latter days because the concept of Christian Providence, with its ideal of passive acceptance, was felt to be completely antithetical to the old heroic ideal of outfacing one's *wyrd*. A more likely explanation may be found in the vanishing of Anglo-Saxon monks with literary tastes and the leisure to write down or copy for posterity the native poetry available to them.

FURTHER READINGS

Anderson, George K., *The Literature of the Anglo-Saxons*, Princeton, N. J.: Princeton University Press, 1949.

Blair, Peter H., *An Introduction to Anglo-Saxon England*, Cambridge, Eng.: University Press, 1956.

Deanesly, Margaret, *Augustine of Canterbury*, London: Thomas Nelson and Sons, 1964.

————, *The Pre-Conquest Church in England*, 2nd ed., London: Adam and Charles Black, 1963.

Duckett, Eleanor Shipley, *Alfred the Great*, Chicago, Ill.: University of Chicago Press, 1956.

Green, Charles, *Sutton Hoo, The Excavation of a Royal Ship Burial*, London: Merlin, 1963.

Greenfield, Stanley B., *A Critical History of Old English Literature*, New York: New York University Press, 1965.

Malone, Kemp, "The Old English Period (to 1100)," in *A Literary History of England*, Albert C. Baugh *et al.*, New York: Appleton-Century-Crofts, 1948.

Sutton Hoo Ship Burial, The, A Provisional Guide, London: The Trustees of the British Museum, 1947.

Trevelyan, George M., *History of England*, Vol. I, Garden City, N. Y.: Doubleday & Company, 1953.

Whitelock, Dorothy, *The Beginnings of English Society*, Harmondsworth, Middlesex: Pelican Books, 1952.

II. Social and Religious Backgrounds: Middle English Period

For the student of literature, the important facts of pre-Conquest history are the assimilation of Christianity by the Anglo-Saxons and the evolution, in the face of repeated invasions and devastation, of a more or less homogeneous nation. The Middle English period, 1100 to 1500, although sufficiently turbulent, witnessed no great invasions after the Normans and no massive settlements of alien peoples. The literature of these four centuries seems to have responded most significantly to changes in the social structure—in particular, to the rise and fall of the feudal order—and to the emergence of a Christian civilization that was in the cultural mainstream of Western Europe and at the same time specifically English in its relatively democratic basis. As in the preceding chapter, such conditions and forces can be delineated here only in broad strokes and with a minimum of attention to the reigns of individual kings and to the history of institutions.

Significant changes in the feudal organization of English society may be explained by reference to a few historical landmarks and developmental stages. The first of these is the systematic introduction by William the Conqueror (1066-1087) of land tenure by knight service, and the formalizing of all other feudal obligations. By the last year of William I, all positions of authority in state and Church had passed into the hands of Frenchmen who were accustomed to such a system. Thus, when enforced by able and ruthlessly vigorous rulers, like William I and William II (1087-1100), these innovations resulted in a powerful state, organized for war.

A second and probably inevitable development was a revolt of the baronage, the occasion being the claims on the throne advanced by Robert of Normandy against his younger brother Henry I (1100-1135). Henry, only slightly less strong than his predecessors, was at length able to suppress his barons, but the warfare illustrates the basic instability of feudalism. The accession of Stephen (1135-1154), a man of weak character whose lineal right to the kingship was dubious at best, was the signal for widespread insurrection both in England and Normandy. The barons took up arms against their ruler both on their own behalf and in support of the rival claims of the Empress Matilda, daughter of Henry I, and now wife of Geoffrey of Anjou. The *Saxon Chronicle* speaks movingly about the hardships and tortures inflicted on the poor men of the realm during the nineteen terrible winters while Stephen was king. The choice of Stephen's successor, Henry II (1154-1189), son of Matilda, was a fortunate one. Again, England had a ruler strong-willed enough to discipline the baronage and to cause them to dismantle the strongholds, or adulterine castles, they had built in defiance of the crown during the previous reign. Part of Henry II's success is attributed to his habit of consulting the barons on important issues. In 1164 and again in 1166, councils of barons issued legislation that very materially strengthened the king's hand against recalcitrant subjects. One important measure, for example, extended his legal authority by defining the relationship of royal to ecclesiastical courts. Profound differences in this matter underlay the prolonged struggle between Henry and his famous archbishop and chancellor Thomas à Becket. The other action was a nationwide assize of military service which asserted the principle that under-tenants' duties to the king overrode their obligations to their immediate feudal superiors.

The third stage, embracing the late twelfth and the first two-thirds of the thirteenth century, witnesses the efforts made by a series of kings to wield the authority granted them by the traditions of the Conqueror and by the enactments under Henry II. The royal prestige established by the line of rulers beginning with the Angevins survived the absentee reign of Richard I (1189-1199) largely because of the service of able justiciars, William Longchamp and Hubert Walter. King John (1199-1216), on the other hand, was less fortunate; moreover, he was conspicuously lacking in the personal qualities necessary for maintaining his father's policies. His loss of the Duchy of Normandy to Philip Augustus of France in 1204, his conflict with Pope Innocent III which led to his submission and even his meek acceptance of England's status as a Papal fief, and his demand for scutage, or money payments in lieu of knight service, for carrying on an unpopular war in France brought about a general rebellion on the part of his chief tenants. Out of the unrest came Magna Carta, signed in 1215, which spelled out the reciprocal obligations of the crown and the baronage. John's successor, Henry III (1216-1272), was a pious, well-intentioned man, but he too proved unfitted for the times, allowing the Holy See to pilfer the national Church and providing lavishly for foreign kinsmen of his queen. With the connivance of the pope, he was able to set aside the Provisions of Oxford, forced on him by an impatient baronage in 1258 who sought thereby to establish a reform commission. Civil war followed, which, after the temporary triumph of Simon de Montfort, ended in a settlement in the late 1260's recognizing the royalists as victorious.

Henry II is said to have spoken no English, Richard the Lion Hearted had scant time for his kingdom, and the main theater of John's activities and military humiliations was France. Henry III, on his part, venerated the memory of Edward the Confessor and, despite his predilection for foreigners, seems to have regarded himself as an Englishman. Indeed, a number of thirteenth-century developments give evidence of a resurgence of native English civilization. A drift away from villeinage and the formation of a middle class of freemen may be discerned, and the towns and boroughs enjoyed an increase in population and in prestige, even achieving the dignity of representation in the King's Council. As economic activity increased, trade and craft gilds were organized and, under gild leadership, the towns began to govern themselves. Many of these advances came about as wartime concessions by kings who needed liberal grants of money. During the thirteenth century also, the universities at Oxford and Cambridge emerged as organized seats of learning, and the Franciscan and Dominican friars came into England in significant numbers. Further, in the late twelfth and the thirteenth century we should note the reappearance of a recorded literature in English and a rather abrupt falling-off of writings in Anglo-Norman.

The period 1272 to the end of the English Middle Ages, the fourth stage, saw the maturing of the movements just mentioned and the dismantling of the feudal order. During the reigns of the three Edwards, covering the first half of this period, further authority over the feudatories was granted to the crown. Under Edward I (1272-1307), the statute of Mortmain decreed that further transfers of lay holdings to the "dead hand" of the Church could be made only with royal permission. In view of the fact that the secular hierarchy of the Church and the religious houses together owned almost one-third of English lands, this act came none too soon. In 1290, another law provided that, upon the alienation of an estate, new grants of tenure by knight service could be made only by the king. In effect, this law contributed to the dissolution of feudal ties because it concentrated military power in royal hands. Edward I's wars against the Welsh, Scots, and French were expensive, and, despite his impressive victories, he had to appeal for funds to the so-called Model Parliament of 1295, an assemblage of magnates, of two knights from every shire, and two representatives from each borough.

The misrule and the great losses under Edward II (1307-1327) were more than redressed by Edward III (1327-1377), who recaptured Scotland and many of the old French holdings of the crown. In Edward's last years, and especially after the death of the Black Prince in 1376, the French made broad advances in Gascony and elsewhere. The English decline continued under the unhappy rule of Richard II (1377-1399), who was deposed in order to make way for the Lancastrian, Henry IV (1399-1413). Henry IV, a firm ruler, owed his accession directly to Parliament, a circumstance that made him far more responsive to the will of that body than his predecessors needed to be. English fortunes soared once more under Henry V (1413-1422), beginning with the great victory at Agincourt in 1415; and, under the regency of the Duke of Bedford, the young Henry VI was crowned King of France in 1431. The high water mark of English power on the Continent had been reached, however. The appearance of a strong Dauphin and of Jeanne d'Arc heralded a return of French energy, and by 1453 only Calais remained to the English of all their former possessions. The Hundred Years' War was at last over only to be succeeded by the War of the Roses, opening in 1455. Edward IV (1461-1483), successor to the mad Henry VI, managed to rule with little dependence on Parliament after his initial troubles with supporters of the deposed king. The cloud of hatred and suspicion which accompanied the accession of Richard III (1483-1485) paved the way for Henry Tudor who, achieving a victory over the unenthusiastic royalist forces at Bosworth Field in 1485, was at once recognized as king. Parliament seems to have been moved to this action more by the will of the commoners than by the legal force of Henry's claim.

Several forces combined in the fourteenth and fifteenth centuries further to loosen the bonds of feudal society in

England. The success of the *curia regis* in securing concessions from kings who needed funds for their war chests
served as a check on absolutism. And when the Council
included representatives of the boroughs, the voice of the
commons came to be heard, a factor that worked steadily
against the old-time feudal control. A great growth in trade,
and especially of the new wool industry, led to further
prosperity of the towns and to a very rapid expansion in the
ranks of freemen at the expense of the villein class in the
manorial villages. The latter trend was greatly accelerated
by the effects of the Black Death which, in four visitations
in the fourteenth century—1348, 1349, 1362, and 1369
—reduced the population of the kingdom by at least one-
third. Owing to the scarcity of labor thus created, wages
rose and humble tenant farmers and cottagers left the land
and migrated to the towns and boroughs by the thousands.
By the end of the fifteenth century, defections of this sort
as well as commutations of labor service by money payments and the wholesale enclosure of lands for sheep walks
led to the virtual disappearance of villeinage in England.
The prominence of the now greatly augmented middle
class, already prosperous and quite capable of making its
influence felt, marks the end of feudal society.

It seems likely that the lowered prestige of the Church
during the fourteenth century also contributed to the relax-
ing of old bonds and to the rise of nationalist feeling. The
cause for decreased veneration was, first, the "Babylonish
Captivity," or the "captivity" of the Papacy by the French,
1308-1378, when the popes held court at Avignon. Second,
immediately succeeding the return of the Papacy to Rome,
rival groups of cardinals elected two popes, and the "Great
Schism," lasting from 1378 to 1417, ensued. The English
crown enforced allegiance to the popes in Rome during
these latter years although the reasons for the choice were
political rather than religious.

The foregoing historical sketch will assume more direct
relevance to the study of literature when supplemented by
some attention to the composition and size of the several

social classes, of the influence of the Church, and of the growth of educational opportunities. We are interested both in throwing light on the general cultural conditioning of writers and also in the emergence of sizeable numbers of people literate in English and sufficiently above the subsistence level to furnish reading audiences for the literature of the period. Further, an understanding of the social structure sometimes bears directly on our reading of literary works. For example, Piers Plowman, as he appears in the opening of one of the greatest of medieval poems, is of villein status, as the reference to his plowing his "half acre" makes evident. Again, the wide social spectrum represented by the Canterbury Pilgrims, from the gentry (the Knight, Squire, and Prioress) down to unfree tenants (the Plowman and possibly the Reeve), underlies no small part of Chaucer's irony, humor, and wisdom.[1]

As already indicated in the preceding chapter, the population of England exclusive of Wales and Scotland stood at about 1,100,000 in 1086, an unbelievably small number by modern standards. The twelfth and thirteenth centuries were a period of prosperity and increase, and in 1348, just before the onset of the great Plague, the inhabitants, according to J. C. Russell, totalled 3,700,000. The appalling death rate of the following three decades reduced that number to 2,200,000, and no large increment may be charted until after 1450. One index to the deadliness of the bubonic plague is that life expectancy at birth, which is calculated to have been 31 years in the final decades of the thirteenth century, fell to 17 years in the period 1348-1375.[2]

A rough breakdown of the population by class in the fourteenth century runs as follows: the greater and lesser baronage, including the important comital families down to simple knights, probably did not embrace much more than 1 per cent of the total. All categories of persons in religion, a subject to be treated later, accounted for perhaps 2 per cent. The two remaining classes, then, the freemen and the villeins together, made up at least 97 per cent. The freemen, a highly miscellaneous group, consisted of burgesses in trades and crafts, yeoman farmers, and wage earners. The villeins were nearly all farmers who held their meager strips of farm land on terms of labor services to their lords. As explained earlier, a considerable proportion of the Anglo-Saxon peasants had been forced into bondage by adverse conditions. The status of these people altered little under the Norman kings, but later circumstances favored the passage of villein families into the ranks of freemen. At the close of the Middle Ages, in fact, the new class had absorbed virtually all persons of unfree status.

In the mid-fourteenth century before the full effects of the Plague had been felt, about 50 per cent of the populace still lived under some form of servitude. Class distinctions were far from absolute: some men legally classed as villeins held not only their ancestral strips in the fields of the home manor for which they performed week-work and other services but also parcels of freehold land. Freemen, on the other hand, are occasionally found to have come into possession of villein holdings. At a more exalted level, younger sons of gentlemen sometimes served an apprenticeship and became merchants or tradesmen.

A notion of how the mass of medieval Englishmen lived may be inferred from the records. Most of the new freemen dwelt in the towns and boroughs. Although rather loosely applied, the term "borough" generally designated a town that had secured relief from certain feudal restrictions and obligations by a charter granted by the crown or the local lord. One of the common privileges allowed the boroughs was that of holding market fairs; also they maintained their own municipal government, erected city walls, and in later years sent representatives to Parliament. The larger communities of medieval England—those of more than 500 population—were normally boroughs, although some quite large places remained under the control of lords, lay or ecclesiastical. Poll tax returns of 1377, immediately after a visitation of the Plague, indicate the existence of 46 boroughs with populations ranging from the 35,000 recorded for London to 759 for Dartmouth. Besides London, the ranking towns were York, Bristol, Plymouth, Coventry, Norwich, Salisbury, Lynn, Colchester, Gloucester, and Boston. The largest of these, York, a cathedral city, of course, numbered well over 10,000, but the remainder ranged from 8,000 downward. Many towns were of ancient origin; the newer communities tended to grow up around the diocesan or archdiocesan centers, the two universities, the greater monastic houses, the seats of important lords, and hubs of trade and transportation. Sometimes they grew from an amalgamation of manorial villages.[3]

More than nine out of ten inhabitants throughout medieval times were rural—that is, they dwelt in thousands of tiny villages, most of them located on manors. Just as in Anglo-Saxon times, relatively few families lived on isolated homesteads. The villagers fell into several categories: First, the villeins, the most numerous group through the fourteenth century, dwelt in one-room cottages lining the village street and farmed their thirty or so half-acre strips scattered about the two or three great fields of the manor. In return for hereditary possession of their land, the villeins performed their allotted week-work for the lord—sheepshearing, sowing, threshing, wood-cutting, and the like, paid fines on the marriage of a daughter to a man who was not a dependent of the home manor, attended the lord's hallmote, and carried out other customary obligations, including payment of Church tithes. For misdemeanors and most crimes these tenants were subject to the jurisdiction of the lord's courts. Of the freemen who lived on the land, the most considerable were sometimes called franklins and maintained the state of a squire. Most village freemen, however, had holdings no larger than those of villeins. Indeed, some of them were very poor, being dependent on the wages they could get from holders of virgates, who might be of villein status, or as servants in the lord's manor house. Still a third group of villagers consisted of cotters, who held only a cottage and little if any manorial land and, like the poorest freeholders, worked for wages.

The diminution of the villein class, as already indicated, went on apace, especially after the middle of the fourteenth century. Some men achieved freedom or a measure of freedom through purchase or the payment of money to the lord, but a villein might also escape to a borough or royal demesne, or achieve liberty by entering the service of the Church. It has been said that no particular sense of indignity attached to the status of the English villein, but this view is difficult to reconcile with the resentment expressed by villagers when called "villein" and with the wholesale exodus from villeinage in the late Middle Ages.

The differences between the rural villages and the towns and boroughs must have been considerably greater than any ostensible present-day parallels would lead us to suspect. The narrowness and laboriousness of the villager's everyday existence may scarcely be exaggerated; for most, the manor constituted the whole of the universe. Relief from monotony was found only in the occasional church-ales, Rogationtide processions, plowing feasts, mummings, Michaelmas harvest festivals, and military service. There were virtually no schools, and the parish church was the sole cultural institution. Village records provide a most useful picture of the peasant's daily round. In the township of Hitchin, a royal manor in Hertfordshire, the medieval community is found to have consisted of some forty-eight property holders, most of them villein tenants and cotters. The freemen either rented demesne lands or earned wages as servants. The services, payments, and obligations owed by the villeins were heavy, their week-work amounting to as much as three days each week. In addition, there were tasks called boon-work assigned on special request, the kirkshot or hearth-penny, Easter dues, fines on the marriage of a daughter or on proof of her incontinence, the obligation to use the lord's mill and attend his court, and the solemn undertaking not to leave the land.[4]

In picturing a hypothetical manorial village of about 1320, to which he gives the name of "Belcomb," H. S.

Bennett provides an admirably detailed account of the cropping system, the pasturage of cattle, and numerous other aspects of "high farming" in medieval England. He also comments on the often severe restrictions of the villein's life, the villein's resentment of his unfree status, and the widespread movement to obtain freedom from reluctant lords, lay and ecclesiastical. Bennett's fine description of a medieval village bears quotation:

As the light strengthened, bit by bit the village became visible, and the confused medley, in which here a roof and there a bit of wall stood out, began to arrange itself as a narrow street with flimsy houses dotted about in little groups. In the centre of it all the stone-built church loomed up high and very new-looking above everything about it, and made the peasants' houses appear small and insignificant. On closer view, the village was seen to radiate from the church and down each of the winding ways that led up to it the peasants had built their homes. There they stood, some neat and trim, with their thatched roofs and roughly finished walls in good repair, while others were dilapidated and showed evident signs of neglect and decay. The larger houses stood a little back from the lane, so that the ground in front of each of them was roughly enclosed and set with young cabbage, onions and parsley, and here and there a few herbs were growing along the sides of the pathway to the house. Most of them had a rudely constructed shed or lean-to at the back of the house, and running away from this stretched another enclosed piece of ground. This was mainly broken up and planted with vegetables, and both here and in the rough grass beyond there were a few apple and cherry trees. At the bottom of the garden where it ran down to the stream the pigs had their styes, and any villager fortunate enough to own a cow tethered it there in among the rankly growing grass. Smaller houses had meagre plots about them, with sparse room for cabbage or onion, and only rarely a pig or a few fowls.[5]

Another historian's reconstruction of the actual village of Wigston Magna in Leicestershire is even more circumstantial. Larger and more affluent than most villages, Wigston consisted of 83 households at Domesday and 110 to 120 in 1377. At an average of three to four persons per family, the population in the fourteenth century must have approached 400. Considerable attention is given to the holdings of peasant families, bond and free, to the kinds of obligations due the two lords who divided the village between them, to taxes, and to other legal matters. The craftsmen and tradesmen in Wigston Magna—a smith, wheelright, carpenter, butcher, miller, baker, and tailor— seem to have carried on their several occupations while at the same time farming their hereditary villein holdings. From inventories in wills and other documents, it is shown that most of the houses were miserable one-room huts with mud walls and thatched roof. Household utensils, bedding, clothing, and tools were meager and crude in the extreme.[6]

Without a consideration of the highly important role of the parish church, a subject to be taken up presently, the foregoing picture of village life is far from complete. It is clear, however, that villagers reared in mud hovels and bound to the soil by an inexorable routine of labor and services would long not only for personal freedom but also for a chance to share in the excitement and amenities of town life about which reports must have reached them. Only the more intelligent, vigorous, and daring among the villeins found their way into the towns, either through legitimate manumission or through escape. There, they would stare at the activity of the great street markets, the rows of craftsmen's and merchants' booths with their display of rich wares, the ships at the docks, the ceremonial processions of aldermen or liveried members of a merchant's company, and perhaps even at the pageants of a mystery play.

In its social and economic aspects, town life must have seemed strange and frightening to the newly arrived countryman who needed to find a means of livelihood. The social stratification which had begun to appear in the thirteenth century was peculiar to the towns, being the result of the control exercised by the most important gilds or companies. Apart from members of the aristocracy who might own town dwellings, and the clergy, such as a bishop's household, the town inhabitants were either citizens or non-citizens, the latter being subdivided into "foreigns," or Englishmen who had not achieved municipal citizenship, and "aliens," or immigrants from the Continent. In London, where full development was reached earlier than in other towns, were to be found many of the aristocracy, an indefinitely large group of court officials, and numerous clergy and lawyers. The companies of drapers, fishmongers, goldsmiths, grocers, haberdashers, mercers, skinners, vintners, and the like, from whose members the aldermen, sheriff, and mayor were chosen, wielded great authority, both economic and political. Each company exercised wide regulatory powers over its membership with respect to retail prices, quality standards, conditions of apprenticeship, and the general conduct of affairs within the municipal walls. Moreover, a man gained citizenship, the freedom of the city, through the sponsorship of a company. Membership in a particular company did not, however, necessarily indicate a man's actual occupation, for many a shrewd gildsman engaged or invested in enterprises far removed from his original calling.[7]

The companies normally served as benevolent and religious associations for the good of their membership, choosing a patron saint whose feast day would be duly observed, endowing chantry priests to celebrate obits for their loved ones, and sometimes building an aisle on a church housing a chapel for their exclusive use. Master craftsmen and merchants with their own establishments trained apprentices for substantial fees. Bondsmen or recent bondsmen from the country occasionally became apprentices, but the Mercers stipulated in 1404 that they would accept no apprentice "who was not a freeman born and a freeman's son." Without special assistance, few of the young men fresh from their villein status could have found the money required of an apprentice. The greater companies honored their most wealthy and eminent masters by permitting them to wear a resplendent livery on special occasions. The rank and file of company membership, of course, was made up of hard-working small shop owners and journeymen. The non-citizens in the towns, foreigns and aliens, worked mainly as servants in manufacturing and business establishments, although some humble crafts were open to them. The most prominent businessmen were treated with respect by the king and the aristocracy; Edward III, in fact, was received as a brother of the powerful Skinner's Company of London. In the fifteenth century, the line between the hereditary gentry and the older merchant families became thin without by any means vanishing. A numerical estimate of the mercantile and industrial class in a given medieval town at a particular time is difficult to establish. One historian has arrived at the figure of 33,000, counting families, apprentices, and retainers, for London in 1501, perhaps half the total population of the city at that date.[8] It is not implausible to think that in the other far less diversified towns the proportion of people making up the organized commercial class was at least as great.

Many merchant families were noted for their wealth, such as the Chicheles, Cavendishes, and Walworths of London. From such families the aldermen and the other municipal officers were recruited; moreover, some of them assumed coats of arms and achieved an occasional knighthood in the fifteenth century as evidence of their social rise. These families often lived in fine quarters built above their narrow, street-level shops, although not until the very end of the Middle Ages was there a marked tendency to provide more than dormitory arrangements for family and servants.

Furniture too seems to have been meager, but certainly there was a degree of ostentation in the use of colorful tapestries, glass windows, silver plate, fur-trimmed gowns, jewelry, food, and drink. In contrast, the poor of the towns lived from hand to mouth in exceedingly crowded and insanitary tenements.

The ability to read and write was clearly a necessity for merchants of any consequence, although such an accomplishment was perhaps less important to men in the crafts, such as sawyers or barbers, and to those who did not rise above a journeyman's status. That the mercantile class did become literate at least in English, and many of them in French and Latin as well, is readily demonstrable although nothing approaching literacy statistics are available. In the mid-fifteenth century, court records—specifically, depositions of witnesses who were required to state whether or not they could read and write—are said by some to suggest that 50 per cent of male Londoners at that time could be called literate, a figure that seems very high. Certainly, this proportion for the fifteenth century would include all the barely literate, and this optimistic estimate would have to be scaled down in speaking of towns other than London. Moreover, the rate for the preceding two centuries must have been notably smaller than in 1450.

How the merchant class learned to read and write is a difficult question. Formal education was in the hands of religious organizations and, at the elementary or grammar school level, was concerned almost exclusively with the teaching of Latin. It is plain that some merchants, eager to adjust their cultural aspirations to those of the aristocracy, sent their sons to grammar schools and even to the universities in the fourteenth and fifteenth centuries, and that a few of those so educated entered the family business. But the great majority of young men who passed through an apprenticeship and became indentured must have learned their three R's in more humble and utilitarian institutions. Such elementary English schools were conducted, on a fee basis, by occasional priests, especially chantry priests, and scriveners likewise appear to have provided training in writing. Arithmetic, accounting, and French were also available under such auspices, the latter because French continued to be much used in business and personal correspondence. The daughters of landed and merchant families were not altogether neglected, sometimes receiving a smattering of education from governesses and in nunnery schools.[9]

In the merchant class dwelling in the forty-odd boroughs, but particularly in London, we at last have an audience of literate laity. This is not to say that all who joined the rapidly growing middle class turned at once to the cultivation of *belles lettres*. On the other hand, books figure with increasing frequency in wills and inventories beginning in the fourteenth century. A cult of respectability is probably responsible for the preponderance in these records of primers, books of hours, devotional and doctrinal treatises, and similar religious books. But we find a grocer in the 1390's who owned two books labeled "romances," and a library was established at a fairly early date in the London gildhall. In Henry Lovelich, a member of the Skinner's Company of London in the first part of the fifteenth century, we have an excellent example of a merchant of bookish enthusiasms although of very slight talent. As a compliment to Harry Barton, a distinguished fellow gildsman who had been Sheriff and twice Lord Mayor of London, Lovelich undertook the huge task of translating great sections from the Old French Arthurian Vulgate into some 50,000 bad English couplets. The result in two parts, entitled *The Holy Grail* and *Merlin*, is preserved in what may be the holograph manuscript. Lovelich's translation errors, some of them amusing to the reader, reveal his inadequacy in French, and the quality of the whole is decidedly inferior to that of the original. Nevertheless, we are grateful for the light which this amateur work casts on the interests of Lovelich's class.

William Caxton is the great example of the merchant-*littérateur* of the fifteenth century. Having retired from his business as a mercer in the Low Countries, probably the city of Bruges, in about 1476, he moved to London and resumed there the printing and publishing activity he had begun on the Continent. Even had he not taken up the art of printing, Caxton would almost certainly have left us a record of his literary interests, for he was an active translator from French and Flemish. Caxton found patrons for his work, most of them apparently of the aristocracy, and in other respects too reveals the typical successful merchant's penchant for aligning himself with the gentry, as in his famous preface to Malory's *Morte Darthur* in which he urges a return to the nobility and the ancient virtues of knighthood. At the same time, we know that he translated and printed *The Mirrour of the World* at the instance of a goldsmith, Sir Hugh Brice. Moreover, the ninety cannily-selected titles that came from his press undoubtedly represent a cross section of the literary preferences of both the merchants and the upper strata of society.[10]

Lovelich and Caxton, to be sure, lived at the very close of the Middle Ages. It is clear, however, that they were not the first members of the middle class to leave their mark on English literature. Many of the manuscripts in which the literature of the fourteenth century is known to us appear to be the product of early "bookshops" which maintained a staff of copyists and translators. A large number of the manuscripts of the *Canterbury Tales* and also the famous Auchinleck miscellany, for example, were "shop-made." [11] Even though records are lacking, the likelihood that some of these manuscripts were commissioned by merchants is not to be overlooked. At least in the capacity of consumers and probably of patrons as well, the rising middle class of the towns of England played a part of great importance in literary history. It must be remembered too that Chaucer's father was a vintner and a man who had achieved a position of considerable importance before the middle of the fourteenth century.

A large part of the Old English literature known to us, as has been indicated in the preceding chapter, bears the imprint of composition or at least of reworking by clerics.

Some of the traditional poetry must have lived for some time in the memory of minstrels before being written down, sometimes with Christian modifications or interpolations by priests or monks. In addition to the always uncertain and indefinable listening audiences, this literature, once committed to writing, would also be available to the reading public, which in Anglo-Saxon times could be only the clerkly class. The situation in which clerics, through their monopoly on learning, controlled in large measure the output of vernacular literature and simultaneously furnished, along with the few literates among the laity, the readers of that literature, persisted into the post-Conquest period. Gradually, and then by the fourteenth century very rapidly, the rising middle class came not only to add considerably to the potential reading public but it further exerted an influence on literary tastes. Very likely, the presence of this new element encouraged the composition and the writing down of purely secular literature, such as tales, lyrics, and some romances, that might in earlier years have never been composed or if composed allowed to perish. On the other hand, vernacular literature may not be said suddenly to have become secularized. The merchants of the towns tended to favor moral-didactic writings even when they read fabliaux and romances. But more importantly, all education above the elementary level, the grammar school in particular, was and continued to remain under the aegis of the Church and was oriented toward the preparation of priests. Again, from the parish church itself flowed an endless stream of dogma and moral exhortation. These Christian influences were of primary significance to all aspects of medieval culture, and an understanding of them is crucial to a student of Middle English literature.

In the centuries following the Conquest, the Church grew at a more rapid rate than the population. Well before the fourteenth century, there was a total in round numbers of 9,500 parishes in the 18 dioceses of England. Only about 500 parishes lay within the 40 to 50 towns—the walls of medieval London alone enclosed about 100—leaving a total of 9,000 rural parishes. These parishes, at least in many parts of England, were coextensive with manorial boundaries, but they varied greatly in extent, some containing two villages, and the number of parishioners likewise varied from possibly 50 to 200 or 300. Most of the town churches generally served greater numbers.

Data as to the numbers of persons who entered the Church in one professional capacity or another are of interest chiefly by way of illustrating the penetration of all levels of society by religion. In the thirteenth and fourteenth centuries, the members of the secular hierarchy and of the religious orders together represented a proportion of the population fifteen to twenty times larger than the proportion of the clergy of all denominations in present-day England. The Poll Tax returns of 1377, after the worst ravages of the Plague had been sustained by Churchmen as well as laity, reveal the existence of 8,000 holders of secular benefices, 11,000 men and women in the regular orders, and possibly 16,000 unbeneficed clerks.[12]

As commonly used by English writers, the term "clerk" (Latin *clericus*) requires a word of explanation. Primarily, the term applied to men in minor orders—that is, those who, planning to become priests, had taken first tonsure and one or more of the minor orders of porter, lector, exorcist, or acolyte. The general practice of the Church was to ordain to priesthood only those who could be provided with a benefice or cure of souls carrying an income. While awaiting the award of a benefice from their bishops or other patrons, young clerks commonly took employment requiring some education, as Chaucer indicates in his account of the Clerk of Oxford. At the time of their institution to benefices, clerks were expected to have reached the grade of "deacon," the second of the major orders of subdeacon, deacon, and priest. Not until they achieved priesthood, of course, could they administer all the sacraments. Some of the 16,000 unbeneficed clerks polled in 1377 were young men awaiting benefices and ordination, but a great many of the others must long since have decided to remain in worldly employment in a court of law, the household of a great lord, the king's exchequer, or a more humble secretarial post. In addition, a good part of the several thousand students at Oxford and Cambridge universities were classified as clerks. Numerous students were actually in minor and sometimes in major orders, not a few being holders of benefices. But by custom, even lay students could wear the tonsure and clerical garb and could claim privilege of clergy, or judgment in ecclesiastical rather than civil courts.

The term "clerk" further included the regulars (those living under a rule, Latin *regula*) in monasteries, friaries, priories, and nunneries, and the whole body of secular priesthood as well. And by an even greater extension, the title embraced the whole of the learned and professional class—lay professors and theologians, physicians, and lawyers. In an account of England written by a Venetian in about 1500 occurs the statement that, since few Englishmen were addicted to letters, any man with learning, even though a layman, was called a clerk.[13]

Service in the Church was theoretically open to all, and a surprising degree of democracy in this respect seems actually to have prevailed in England. During the twelfth century, the great age of monasticism, the monasteries attracted members of the ruling and the more affluent families in some number although later they suffered a decline in prestige and came commonly to draw upon the lesser people of the realm, just as did the four orders of friars, or wandering, mendicant preachers—the Franciscans, Dominicans, Austins, and Carmelites. The women who entered nunneries tended always to come from the upper classes, probably because of the frequent requirement of a dowry. The ranks of the monks were swelled by the adoption of a monastic rule by the clergy staffing more than one-half of the cathedral churches. Such chapters were known as priories, the monk who served as the superior, and also as second in authority to the bishop, being called the prior. The clergy at the remaining "secular" cathedrals were known as canons secular. Similar "colleges" of canons secular were to be found at the several collegiate churches which, like Southwell in Nottinghamshire and Beverley Minster in Yorkshire, were churches endowed with property for the support of prebends.

Including the chapters at the monastic cathedrals and houses of study at the universities, the communities maintained by the regular orders—the monks, friars, nuns, and a special category of monks known as canons regular—numbered approximately 800 in the thirteenth and fourteenth centuries. Some were great baronial establishments like the Benedictine abbey at Bury St. Edmunds, whose abbot ruled some 80 monks and administered 170 manors, but at the other end of the scale were the very small monasteries and cells consisting of a mere handful of religious living in great poverty. The houses of friars, located for the most part in the towns, varied in size, and the canonries were a little smaller on the average than the monasteries. The great number of men and women in the regular orders as well as the fairly even geographical distribution of their houses must have ensured a high degree of contact with the lay people, a social fact reflected in literature. Other dealings of the laity and the regular clergy resulted from the circumstance that, by the fourteenth century, the principal revenues and the advowson, or right of supplying the priest, of one-third to one-half of all the parishes in England had passed, generally by gift, from the hands of private landlords to religious houses. The religious houses served, in effect, as corporate rectors of the parishes under their control, taking the greater tithes for their own use and sometimes farming out the glebe, or the farm land designated for the priest's personal support. In return, they provided a hireling priest called a vicar, usually at a pittance. The establishing and regularizing of the vicarage system, in fact, went hand in hand with the appropriation of parishes by religious houses and brought various evils in its train.

In contrast to the regular orders, the men entering the secular hierarchy were fairly representative of the social spectrum of medieval England. A few seculars were recruited from titled families, such as the Clares, Nevills, and Bohuns, and such men commonly came into possession of the richer and more important livings, frequently as pluralists, and some achieved the prelacy. In a particularly flagrant instance of family influence, Henry, natural son of Henry II, was consecrated Bishop of Lincoln at the age of fourteen, and seven years later, despite his demonstrated ignorance and incompetence, he became Archbishop of York. On the other hand, some men of wealth and family who occupied diocesan thrones, such as Melton and Zouche, were entirely worthy of their posts. That aristocratic birth or the wealth of a merchant family was not an indispensable requisite to advancement in the hierarchy is made clear by the careers of a number of notable men who worked their way up from the lowliest origins. Perhaps chief among these are Robert Grosseteste, the great Bishop of Lincoln (1235-1253), and Robert de Insula, Bishop of Durham (1274-1283). Occasionally bishops and archbishops were drawn from the regular orders, although after the twelfth century monk and friar bishops are less frequently encountered. In this category, however, fall such later distinguished prelates as John Peckham, Archbishop of Canterbury (1279-1292), a Franciscan of humble parentage; Simon Langham, who had been monk and prior at Westminster before his elevation to the primacy (1366-1368); and the famous preacher, Thomas Brunton or Brinton, who was a monk before becoming Bishop of Rochester (1372-1389). Another index to the social backgrounds of the higher clergy is that two-thirds of the bishops in the fourteenth century are said to have been university graduates.

The inferior clergy—the thousands of poor vicars and their assistants, the chantry priests and singers, and the domestic chaplains—emerged, by and large, from the poorer classes, not excepting the bondsmen. Since canon law forbade the admission to orders of men in unfree condition, sons of serfs were obliged before ordination to obtain their freedom, normally by payment of a fine to their lords. It goes without saying that priests of humble origins, unless, like Grosseteste, exceptionally fortunate in educational opportunities, were destined to spend their ministry in country vicarages on miserable wages.

The educational requirements for ordination to the priesthood were very broadly formulated. In general, it was stipulated that the candidate must have demonstrated his fitness in morals and learning. This principle was enunciated by the very early (747) English Council of Clovesho and supported by a Biblical quotation: "that he may be able by sound doctrine both to exhort and to convince the gainsayers" (Titus 1:9). Later pronouncements concerning cathedral schools and theological lecturers figure in English councils and bishops' constitutions, and these reflect the legislation of the great ecumenical councils, especially those of 1179 and 1215.[14] The Church showed itself deeply concerned for the moral edification of the laity and to that end urged constantly the need for a better educated and trained clergy.

The basic education for English clergy was provided by grammar schools which sprang up under a variety of auspices, such as cathedral and collegiate churches, university colleges like Merton at Oxford, municipalities, merchant gilds, chantry chapels, and monasteries. William of Wykeham's great foundation at Winchester was, of course, unique in quality and prestige among grammar schools. Pregrammar school training in letters, when not available in the home, seems to have been provided by a parish priest or clerk. Thomas Cranmer, who was born in 1489 and became Henry VIII's Archbishop of Canterbury, studied grammar with a "rude parishe clerke" until the age of fourteen when he went directly to Oxford.[15] Song schools, such as that attended by the little "clergeon" in Chaucer's *Prioress's Tale*, may also have offered some elementary schooling.

The grammar-school curriculum centered on the study of Latin grammar and of a few medieval classics. The pupils assimilated a grammar—the *Ars Minor* of Donatus or the

Doctrinale of Alexander of Villedieu, memorized a number of Psalms, and construed into French (in the latter fourteenth century, into English) such edifying works as the *Distichs of Cato*. In the upper forms, Ovid and Virgil were read. The full course seems often to have required four years, but very few of those who entered could study so long. Not all grammar-school students, especially in later times when merchants' sons were seeking an education, considered themselves destined for the Church. Education of this sort, which was not free, generally speaking, seems to have been available in the boroughs, the cathedral cities, and possibly in a few monasteries. In London alone, several grammar schools are known to have existed in the fourteenth and fifteenth centuries. In the thousands of villages, however, no such institutions were to be found, and the priest or parish clerk who kept school must have been rare.

Relatively few men went on from grammar school to the universities, and those who proceeded to a university degree were even fewer. The preferred position of university graduates and scholars is especially apparent in the numbers of papal provisors, or direct appointments by the Holy See, taken from their ranks in the fourteenth century. In the more important city parishes, the merchant class seems occasionally to have made efforts to install university men as their rectors or vicars.

The existence of a number of grammar schools and theological lecturers, to say nothing of the universities, in the thirteenth and fourteenth centuries encourages one to anticipate a rather well-educated clergy to whom "the road to learning is open" (*via pateat ad doctrinam*). It is true that scholars of great eminence occupied English bishoprics from St. Anselm (1093–1109) to Bradwardine (d. 1349), whom Chaucer mentions with reverence, yet nothing is better documented than the conclusion that the lower clergy of the English Church were staggeringly ignorant. Such a state was universal in the Christian Church, to judge from the ecumenical council of 1215 which ascribes the insufficient education of the priests to their miserable wages. In England, the austere friar Archbishop John Peck-ham, in his *Constitutions* of 1281, discourses on the sub-ject circumstantially in the course of urging his priests to preach on the fundamentals of the faith at least four times per year: "The ignorance of priests casts the people into the pit of error; and the stupidity and naïveté of clerks who are enjoined to instruct minds in the Catholic faith conduces more to error than to doctrine." [16] A similar senti-ment about the priesthood of his own day is voiced by John Gower in his Latin poem, *Vox Clamantis*.[17] The adverse comments by other medieval bishops about the inadequacy of their priests were based on their observation of slipshod ordination examinations and the reports of official visita-tions. For example, in 1220, the Dean of Salisbury took note of a priest of the diocese who was unable to read the Latin of the Vulgate even to the extent of understanding the Gospel for the first Sunday in Advent and was equally helpless in grasping the canon of the Mass, the antiphons, the Divine Office, or any one of the Psalms. Along with ignorance of this sort went a certain amount of immorality, or at least of uncanonical conduct.[18]

Such a state of affairs is not surprising when it is consid-ered how many a young peasant must have entered the clergy. In his vivid account of the village of "Belcomb," H. S. Bennett traces the career of a country boy who, after acting as servant to the parish priest, displayed sufficient aptness or zeal to prompt the priest to teach him reading and singing and to advance him to the status of holy water bearer. Given other evidence of a true vocation, the boy received tonsure and served at Mass. Thereafter he might enroll in a cathedral school, if possible, for an extremely limited grammar-school education, relying for support on the holy water benefice or perhaps gifts from villagers. The possibility of his obtaining a more sophisticated education must have been very slight, and with his small Latin and his apprenticeship in the liturgy he presented himself in due course to the archdeacon and bishop for admission to major orders.[19]

The prestige enjoyed by the medieval priest was considerable, despite his poverty—especially that of a mere vicar or chaplain—and the likelihood that he was of lowly origin and by no means impressively prepared for his office. The honor paid him was not solely owing to the sacerdotal powers conferred on him by his orders, although people bowed low or kneeled as, preceded by bell and cross, he bore the viaticum down the road to the house of a moribund parishioner. It was no doubt partly inspired by the more general authority over the lives of the laity vested in the secular hierarchy. The priest, for example, was duty bound to collect tithes, and he was not always so loath as Chaucer's Parson to enforce their payment by the threat of excommunication. Also expected from the parishioners were gifts in kind on certain feast days, Mass pennies, and death duties, called mortuaries. Further, the clergy could and sometimes did inflict humilating public penance on laymen for moral offenses, not sparing those of rank and influence. In turn, the bishop's power over his parish priests, administered by the archdeacon and ecclesiastical courts, was also very great.

The parish church, whether rural or urban, could be a small, ancient structure, like the eighth-century Saxon church still standing at Escomb in Durham, or a later Norman or Gothic building, large out of all proportion to the parish population. Of the latter, literally thousands are still in service in England. Many churches, consisting originally of a simple nave and chancel, were in the thirteenth and fourteenth centuries transformed into miniature cruciform cathedrals by local magnates who built new aisles and transepts to provide space for chantry chapels and tombs. A prominent feature of the interior was often a group of life-size or nearly life-size colored wooden figures of John, Mary, and angels flanking the cross mounted on the rood beam between the nave and chancel. In the tympanum above the rood figures one often saw a more or less crude painting of the Last Judgment, or "Doom," showing Christ in majesty and the sorting out of souls, in the form of little naked people, between heaven and hell. But even such decorations were probably less noticeable than they would be in a modern church because the interior walls were likely to be covered with murals depicting the Nativity, the Ascension, miracles of the saints, the ladder of salvation, and sometimes the wheel of fortune and trees of vices and virtues. As Canon John Myrc, a Kentishman of the early fifteenth century, remarked in one of his sermons: "ymages and payntours ben lewde menys bokys." [20] The rich designs and colors in the windows completed the effect, although it must be admitted that, especially in country churches, signs of neglect and dilapidation and even of non-ecclesiastical use could be seen. Indeed, some churches served at times as village granaries and even as brew-houses.

The nave was bare of pews, since until the early fifteenth century the congregation, the men on one side and the women on the other, was accustomed to stand when not kneeling. The great families, however, had seats reserved for them in the choir. At the eastern end near the altar rail might be found an eagle lectern, but there was no pulpit. Like seats for the congregation, pulpits did not become common until relatively late when sermons were regularly delivered. Other church furniture—the altar with reredos and hangings, the *sedilia* or chairs for clergy, the *piscina* or basin for liturgical washing, and the credence table—was not unrecognizably different from present-day examples. On the other hand, there were no confessional boxes, even though private auricular confession had been an obligation since the early thirteenth century.

The chief sacerdotal duty of the priest was, of course, the daily celebration of Mass, although parishioners probably appeared in numbers only on Sundays and on feast days. Several minor observances distinguish the medieval from the modern celebration. In the English Church could be seen vestiges of the old offertory procession in which communicants carried their oblations of bread and wine to the altar for consecration. This practice gave way to money offerings, the Mass penny, but the procession was retained. Chaucer's Wife of Bath, it will be recalled, became wrathful if anyone "to the offrynge bifore hire sholde goon." The ancient Kiss of Peace, the *Pax Domini*, was originally passed on from the celebrant and assistants to the congregation. In England, people kissed and passed on an *osculatorium* or *pax-brede*, a paddle-shaped device bearing sacred pictures. References to it appear in English writers like Chaucer and Lydgate. Again, after Sunday Mass, the *eulogia*, or "blessed bread," was distributed. This bread, not to be confused with the Host of the Eucharist, was originally part of the oblation which had been left unconsecrated. It was blessed and cut with a special knife.

As a rule, no opportunity was given for the communion of the layfolk except at Easter, and then the people received after the celebration proper. Annual communion, which was a canonical requirement, represents the culmination of a long decline from the practice of the primitive Church, in which lay communion accompanied every Mass. With infrequent communion the people came to surround the prime sacerdotal function, the "making of Christ," with an aura of wonder. In large communities, men sometimes rushed from one church to another in order to witness as many elevations of the Host as possible and thus to reap a multiplicity of benefits that they were explicitly told, as in John Lydgate's poem, *Merita Missae*, would ensue from watching the priest's communion.

Another priestly duty was the daily recitation or singing of the Hours of the Divine Office, a round of services set forth in the breviary made up of prayers, hymns, antiphons, and Psalms, developed originally for monastic devotions. These services, to which frequent references are made in literature, are distinguished according to the time of celebration: (1) Matins, and (2) Lauds, said in succession very early in the morning; (3) Prime, at 6:00, or somewhat later; (4) Terce, shortly after Prime; (5) Sext, either immediately after Terce or with (6) None, at or near noon; (7) Vespers, at midafternoon; and (8) Compline, at 7:00

or 8:00. In monasteries, the times for the formal observances of the Hours varied from one order to another, as
they do today. In most parish churches, public celebration
of the Hours was confined to Sunday and feast-day Matins,
often called "Uht-Song" or "Dawn Song," and Vespers or
Even Song on Saturdays and Sundays at about 3:00. Only
in larger churches served by a staff of clergy could any substantial part of the Hours be celebrated on a daily basis.
The laity were encouraged to attend the Hours in cathedral
churches and no doubt they were frequently urged to appear at whatever observances there were in their own parishes. That their response left something to be desired may
be inferred from a remark in Robert Mannyng's *Handlyng
Synne*, written at the beginning of the fourteenth century:

> Of matyns ryche men take no kepe
> 3yf þey mowe ryse at tyme of messe.[21]

Probably Even Song was attended largely by the devout
women of the parish.

One of the objectives of the religious reform of the late
twelfth and early thirteenth century was to improve the
guidance provided the laity in faith and morals. To this
end, priests having the cure of souls were enjoined more
strictly than heretofore to preach sermons several times
each year on certain clearly defined elements of the faith,
such as the petitions of the Pater Noster, the articles of the
Creed, the Commandments of the Law and the Gospel,
the works of bodily and spiritual mercy, the virtues, the
seven sins, and the like. The paucity of sermon texts and of
allusions to sermons in the thirteenth century suggests that
this injunction was little better heeded than in earlier
times. Bishop Robert Grosseteste complained that few of
his priests preached or were capable of delivering a sermon.
By the mid-fourteenth century, however, the efforts of prelates and the example set by preaching friars had brought
about a change, for sermons figure rather prominently in
the records. Bishop Thomas Brinton, preacher to the courts
of Edward III and Richard II, has left us a collection of

sermons as have other clerics of the period. It is doubtful that country priests were ever expected by their parishioners to preach frequently, but the often well-educated and articulate clergy in the greater towns, on the other hand, must have taken some pride in their pulpit eloquence.

A second measure by which the Church hoped to bring about a more Christian laity was formulated as follows by Pope Innocent III's great council of 1215:

> Let each of the faithful of either sex, after he has reached the age of discretion, confess alone all his sins to his own priest at least once a year and strive with all his strength to fulfill the penance enjoined on him, receiving reverently the sacrament of Eucharist at least at Easter. . . . Otherwise let him be denied entrance to the church while living and Christian burial when he is dead.[22]

In other words, a new obligation of private auricular confession was imposed on all Christians. The clause requiring the Christian to confess to his own priest was directed against the mendicant friars who for decades had everywhere tended to encroach on the prerogatives of humble parish priests. Experienced as preachers and often widely traveled, the friars invading a country parish easily outshone the local vicar; moreover, they were rumored to give easy absolution, as Chaucer states in his unforgettable portrait of Friar Huberd. The interpretation placed on the new canon tended to make confession into a kind of examination of the penitent's knowledge of doctrine. That is, the priest was admonished to elicit a perfect confession by asking many questions about his parishioner's knowledge and understanding of the same points of doctrine about which sermons were presumably preached, the Pater Noster, Ave Maria, Creed, the vices and virtues, and others. The proper confessing of a penitent became, then, a lengthy process; moreover, a ready and expert grasp of Christian fundamentals was demanded of the priest. To aid him in this respect, priests' manuals were written, either in Latin or, for the use of him who was "not grete clerke" and had "no bokes," in English. Moreover, a very large body of doctrinal and devotional treatises, most of them directed toward helping the Christian make a "good shrift," sprang up for the use of the literate layfolk in the towns. More is to be said about these writings in a later chapter.

Paragons of Christian humility, like Chaucer's "povre persoun," must have been rare even in the Middle Ages. Yet a sizeable proportion of the parish clergy, however scantily prepared, probably carried out liturgical duties conscientiously, remembering to observe the sixty or more feast days in the calendar, and conforming to recognized standards of clerical conduct and dress. Further, even though rebukes on this score by diocesan officials were not lacking, the parish clergy must on the whole have discharged creditably enough such other responsibilities as keeping the secrets of the confession; presenting confirmation candidates to their bishops; visiting the sick; administering alms; collecting tithes; forbidding the grazing of cattle, dancing, and the playing of games in the churchyard and cemetery; and serving their parishioners in a legal capacity or merely as scribes. A great majority of vicars must have accepted without undue complaint the life of poverty to which their niggardly stipends, to say nothing of obligations like paying synodal taxes and maintaining their vestments, condemned them. Indeed, in their day-to-day devotion to duty in the face of handicaps, the secular priesthood must often have presented an edifying contrast to the endowed regulars, such as the lordly cathedral canons and the monastics.

From at least late Old English times through the fifteenth century, then, English society at all levels was subjected to religious influences to a degree for which no modern parallel exists. Commercial prosperity in the towns encouraged the development of urban secularism, to be sure, and the nobles and officialdom in the royal court, and conceivably in a few of the great households, cultivated secular interests, as the popularity in such circles of Chaucer, Gower, and others bears witness. On the whole, however, the cultural domination of the Church was virtually un-challenged. A highly important reason for the unbroken reign of religion was that formal education was conceived of primarily as education for the Church. Of even greater significance for the understanding of literature was the role of the parish priest as typically the sole source of enlighten-ment, at least for some 90 per cent of the population. Be-cause of the canonical responsibilities of the lower clergy, to say nothing about their meager education, the instruction which they gave to their parishioners was largely on the plane of simple dogma. Thus was created a kind of com-munity of belief, in England as in other European coun-tries, to which literary men could appeal with confidence.

FURTHER READINGS

Caiger-Smith, A., *English Medieval Mural Paintings*, Oxford, Eng.: The Clarendon Press, 1963.

Coulton, George G., *Medieval Panorama: The English Scene from Conquest to Reformation*, New York: Meridian, 1955.

———, *Medieval Village, Manor, and Monastery*, New York: Harper and Row, 1960.

———, *Ten Medieval Studies*, Cambridge, Eng.: University Press, 1930.

Cutts, Edward L., *Parish Priests and Their People in the Middle Ages in England*, London: SPCK, 1898.

Dix, Dom Gregory, *The Shape of the Liturgy*, London: Dacre, 1954.

Haskins, Charles Homer, *The Rise of Universities*, Ithaca, N. Y.: Cornell University Press, 1957.

Homans, George Caspar, *English Villagers of the Thirteen Cen-tury*, New York: Russell & Russell, 1960.

Leach, A. F., *The Schools of Medieval England*, New York: The Macmillan Company, 1915.

Lennard, Reginald, *Rural England, 1086-1135: A Study of Social and Agrarian Conditions*, Oxford, Eng.: The Clarendon Press, 1959.

Loomis, Laura Hibbard, "The Auchinleck Manuscript and a Possible London Bookshop of 1330-1340," *PMLA*, LVII (1942), 595-627.

Owst, G. R., *Literature and Pulpit in Medieval England*, Cambridge, Eng.: University Press, 1933.

————, *Preaching in Medieval England: An Introduction to Sermon Manuscripts of the Period c. 1350-1450*, Cambridge, Eng.: University Press, 1926.

Stenton, F. M., *The First Century of English Feudalism*, 1066-1166, Oxford, Eng.: The Clarendon Press, 1932.

Thompson, James Westfall, *The Literacy of the Laity in the Middle Ages*, Berkeley: University of California Press, 1939.

Thorndike, Lynn, "Elementary and Secondary Education in the Middle Ages," *Speculum*, XV (1940), 400-08.

III. The English
Language in the
Middle Ages

The literary texts of the eight centuries just surveyed provide the primary basis for understanding the evolution of the language. That linguistic knowledge is essential to a firm comprehension and appreciation of literature becomes amply clear to any one who studies the major works, such as *Beowulf*, the Prefaces of Alfred, or the poems of Chaucer, in their original forms. It is true that Old English and also very early Middle English will strike the present-day reader as alien tongues which, until he can master the grammar and vocabulary, call for full translation. Later Middle English, except for a few dialects, will be recognizable as his native language which he can read, although perhaps haltingly, with the aid of a glossary. But even before one undergoes the discipline of Old English grammar and Middle English dialectology, he can be made aware of some features of the earlier stages of the English language having a direct bearing on literary expression. The aim of the present chapter is to single out these features for discussion. So forewarned, the reader should be less completely at the mercy of the translators of Old English, and he should also be able to read Middle English with greater certainty and profit.

As a point of departure, it is advisable to give some thought to the problems presented by translations in general. Three centuries ago, John Dryden defended his adaptations from Middle English on the grounds that few, except "some old *Saxon* Friends," could read Chaucer's language so as to understand him perfectly.[1] Today, not many would think they are in touch with the real Chaucer when reading Dryden's "Palamon and Arcite," "The Cock and the Fox," or "The Wife of Bath her Tale," delightful and worthy though they are in their own right. An example of Dryden's manner is supplied by his version of *The Wife of Bath's Tale*. For Chaucer's lines—

> And so bifel it that this kyng Arthour
> Hadde in his hous a lusty bacheler,[2]

a passage hardly requiring the help of an old Saxon friend —Dryden writes:

> It so befel in this King *Arthur's* Reign,
> A lusty Knight was pricking o'er the Plain;
> A Bachelor he was, and of the courtly Train.[3]

As may be seen, Dryden departs little from the sense of his original, but his self-conscious archaisms, such as "pricking o'er the Plain," his other expansions or line fillers, and his careful Restoration rime and meter impart a rather finicky tone that is at odds with the modern perception of Chaucer.

The truism that every age interprets the poetry of the past in its own idiom may be illustrated by much more recent translations. Thus, Sir Theodore Martin's late nineteenth-century rendering of the Middle English *Debate of the Body and the Soul* will seem to anyone familiar with the original thirteenth-century poem almost a ludicrous misrepresentation of its meter, pace, and intentionally brusque tone. The poem opens as follows:

Als*a* i lay in a winteris nyt*b*
   In a droukening*c* bifor þe*d* day,
Vor soþe*e* i sauȝ*f* a selly syt,*g*
   A body on a bere*h* lay.[4]

Martin's elegant Spenserian stanza reads in part:

Once as I lay upon a winter night,
   And chid the laggard coming of the day,
Before my eyes there came a dismal sight,
   That settled there, and would not pass away:
     All on a bier a clay-cold Body lay.[5]

Today, much of the earlier literature of England is available in translations that appeal to us far more than those of Dryden or Martin, yet we would be rash to assume that future generations will remain content with our twentieth-century renderings. All literary translators face virtually insuperable problems. In this connection, Robert Frost's remark to the effect that poetry is that which is lost in translation, and the Italian pun on "translator" and "traitor" (*traduttore, traditore*) are often cited. Some hold that poetry resists anything approaching an adequate rendering in another language to an even greater degree than it resists paraphrase. Of immediate relevance here is that the problem persists even when the source language is not German or Russian or Japanese but simply an earlier stage of the translator's mother tongue. The translations and modernizations which the general reader must use if he is to make the acquaintance of much medieval literature are clearly subject to the same severe limitations that characterize all translations. At the same time, one who understands something of the nature of these limitations and of the evolution of Old and Middle English language and literature should be able to read translations with new insight and sense some of the less readily communicable qualities of medieval expression.

a As.   *b* night.   *c* slumber.   *d* the.   *e* Forsooth.
f saw.   *g* wondrous sight.   *h* bier.

The translator's first task is to discover the message of his original as best he can, and his second is to set it forth in the target language. Both stages would be simple of execution if the original work were perfectly objective and unambiguous, but even the most primitive literature is always otherwise. In determining the "meaning" of a literary text, the translator must consider the highly subjective effects of imagery, rhetorical level, tone, sound patterns, and the like. Further, he must take into account aspects of the whole cultural context of the work before him that will seem foreign to readers of his finished product. All these multi-level perceptions he must somehow convey in another language while simultaneously striving to suggest the external form and meter of the original. Nor, as already indicated, is the difficulty the less when the source language happens to be Old English rather than, say, a Slavic language. The procedure of cognate-substitution, followed occasionally by Ezra Pound in his well-known version of the Old English *Seafarer*,[6] is probably no safer when rendering Old English than when rendering German or French. To translate Old English *stol*, meaning "throne," as "stool" would be a laughable error, and by the same token Old English *aldormon*, a title reserved for high official rank, such as "lord" or "prince," could scarcely be represented by Modern English "alderman," with its sometimes unsavory overtones, at least in American politics.

The axiom that poetry does not become poetry until read aloud is perhaps applicable also to prose literature of the Middle Ages, when the tradition of oral performance was still alive. Beyond attending to classroom explanations, the most efficient way for the student to gain an impression of the sounds of Old English, the rhythm of the alliterative staves, and the intonation of prose is to listen to recordings made by linguistic specialists. All stages in the history of English pronunciation, in fact, are now represented in recordings, and from these much may be learned. The most frequently recorded Old English work is *Beowulf*; one present-day scholar has provided an especially dramatic and

lively reading of the poem to the accompaniment of a harp,
a replica of the famous Sutton Hoo instrument.[7]

What is learned by ear alone about the literary language may usefully be supplemented by a few observations
about a passage from *Beowulf*:

            ne mæg ic her leng wesan.
Hataðheaðomære   hlæw gewyrcean
beorhtne æfter bæle   æt brimes nosan;
se scel to gemyndum   minum leodum
heah hlifian   on Hronesnæsse,   2805
þæt hit sæliðend   syððan hatan
Biowulfes biorh,   ða ðe brentingas
ofer floda genipu   feorran drifað.[8]

These lines may be literally translated as follows:

        I may not remain longer.
Command the battle-renowned ones   to build a
    mound
splendid after the burning   at the sea's headland.
It shall be as a reminder   to my peoples
and tower high   on Hronesness,   2805
so that seafarers   shall afterwards call it
Beowulf's Barrow   when they drive their ships
out of the mists of the floods   from afar.

By keeping in mind a few simple principles, the student can read the above lines for himself with something
like the original pronunciation. That is, the symbols ð and
þ both represent *th*, *æ* is pronounced like the vowel in
"cat," and, in general, the other vowels are sounded much
as they are in modern German or French. For example,
drifað, l.2808, is pronounced "dreeveth," the *i* being given
the same value as in German *Igel* or French *idée*.

It is also possible to acquire some sense of the rhythm
of Old English poetry by observing the caesura or pause,
marked by a space, that divides each line into two parts and
by further recalling that every complete line is read with

four strongly accented syllables, two on either side of the pause. Thus, l. 2803 above would be stressed as follows:

beórhtne æfter bǽle　　æt bŕimes nósan

Of the four accented syllables in this line, the first three begin with the same sound, *b*; that is, they alliterate. A similar pattern may be discerned throughout the passage and, indeed, throughout all Old English poetry. That is, one or both of the stressed syllables in the first half line begin with the same sound, consonant or vowel, as may be heard in accented position in the second half line, thus binding the line into a unit. Alliteration, which Old English shares with poetry in the other old Germanic languages, is a major ingredient of the deliberate and elevated style which characterizes medieval epic. Even in the few lines just quoted, one notes differences in the positioning of the stressed syllables—that is, in the number of unaccented syllables separating the stresses. These differences are far from accidental or haphazard; in actuality, a strictly limited number of rhythmic patterns are used over and over, with attention to variation and to special effects. Even in English poetry of modern times, one can sense at least a far-off reminiscence of the ancient stress patterns.[9]

With respect to meaning, the reader will be able to single out words in the *Beowulf* lines that have remained in the language with very slight change in pronunciation, such as *æfter* ("after"), l. 2803; *æt* ("at"), l. 2803; *þæt* ("that"), l. 2806; *hit* ("it"), l. 2806; and *ofer* ("over"), l. 2808. Still other words become identifiable when the differences in vowel pronunciation are taken into account. Thus *minum*, l. 2804, is only our pronoun "mine." The meaning of *minum leodum* ("to my peoples") is tersely indicated by the dative plural ending *-um* on both pronoun and noun; again, the genitive plural inflection *-a* on the single word *floda* ("of the floods"), l. 2808, conveys a meaning that can be rendered only by a prepositional phrase in Modern English. The use of case endings on such words gave to the

Old English stage of our language a compactness and flexibility of word order that became impossible when the inflections largely disappeared. Word compounding was another feature of Old English as it still is of German. Such a substitute as "battle-renowned ones" for the natural and easy *heaðomære*, l. 2802, sounds cumbersome and affected at best to modern ears.

Of greater significance than such differences, perhaps, is the inherent difficulty of finding an appropriate vocabulary for rendering into another idiom the suggestiveness of the original poetry. The Old English bard or *scop* seems to have been an oral composer in the ancient tradition, and we may assume that in the course of a long and exacting apprenticeship he learned a special poetic vocabulary replete with synonyms and metaphoric compounds and phrases, often called "kennings," for such frequently recurring objects and concepts as "sword," "ship," "warrior," "battle," "valor," and the like. A great many of these old expressions have been lost to the language, such as *brentingas* ("ships"), l. 2807 above; others, especially compounds like "swan-road," "fishes' bath," and "beaker of waves," all figurative expressions for "sea," translate so awkwardly that they lose their poetic heightening. The poets also drew on a rich repertoire of formulaic phrases which would fit readily into an alliterative line. Phrases like *ielda bearnum* ("to the children of men") and *mann-cynnes weard* ("guardian of mankind") often appear, especially in religious poetry, including the so-called *Hymn* of Cædmon. The last line of the *Beowulf* passage quoted above was probably felt to be formulaic; in fact, the phrase *ofer floda genipu* ("out of the mists of the floods") occurs with only a slight substitution somewhat earlier in the poem as *ofer floda begang* ("over the circuit of the waves"), l. 1826. The *scop* could apparently draw ready-made phrases of this type from his capacious memory by way of commentary, or emphasis, or simple expansion of his material.

Of course, only an audience of Anglo-Saxons could

appreciate to the full the sophistication of their poets. They would respond to minor variations in familiar metaphors and formulas just as they would recognize subtle differences in alliteration and in rhythmic patterns. Deprived of such associations, the modern reader is likely to regard the traditional poet's resort to stereotyped compounds and phraseology as indicative of a fatal lack of originality, an impression encouraged by translations in which kennings and other stock expressions stand out as flat and repetitious archaisms.

The user of translations, indeed, can counter such a reaction and participate in a more satisfying way in the experience offered by an Old English poem only to the extent that he grasps some of the untranslatable qualities of the old mode. He may safely assume that the original poem is marked by greater terseness and tighter syntactical structure than is possible in modern poetry. Subtle shifts in rhythm and alliterating sounds and perhaps even the stroking of the harp accompaniment could be counted on to evoke certain responses in the original audiences. Further, the old epithets, kennings, and formulas must have aroused deep associations about which we can only speculate today. In translation, these expressions are likely to become almost totally neutralized. The modern reader, in other words, must exert his imagination in certain well-defined directions if he is to supplement or correct the impression conveyed by present-day versions.

Some common characteristics of translations are illustrated in the contrast offered by two widely used renderings of *Beowulf*. The first translator, the earlier of the two, treats the lines already discussed as follows:

> No longer I tarry.
> A barrow bid ye the battle-famed raise
> For my ashes. 'Twill shine by the shore of the flood,
> To folk of mine memorial fair
> On Hrones Headland high uplifted,   2805

That ocean-wanderers oft may hail
Beowulf's Barrow, as back from far
They drive their keels o'er the darkling wave.[10]

Here we see a painstaking carry-over of the accentual patterns and the alliteration of the original. Nevertheless, one
may justifiably doubt that the author is true to the spirit of
the Old English epic when resorting to such worn and
empty clichés of poetic diction as "mine memorial fair,"
"drive their keels," and "o'er the darkling wave." The
other version is largely free from this tendency:

My hour is come, and my end is near.
Bid warriors build, when they burn my body,
A stately barrow on the headland's height.
It shall be for remembrance among my people
As it towers high on the Cape of the Whale,   2805
And sailors shall know it as Beowulf's Barrow,
Sea-faring mariners driving their ships
Through fogs of ocean from far countries.[11]

In this less literal translation, the accentual character of the
original is suggested rather than copied and there is no undue straining after alliteration. Whatever may be lost so far
as the duplication of sound effects is concerned, the result
is dignified and strong, and to many students it will seem to
read more easily and naturally than the earlier rendering.

In general, prose literature, since it depends less heavily than poetry on subtleties of allusion, imagery, and
meter, lends itself much more satisfactorily to translation.
Extant Old English prose at times approaches the simplicity of modern casual conversation, as in the following sentence from Ælfric's sermon "The Assumption of St. John
the Apostle":

"Iohannes, cum to me: tima is þæt þu mid ðinum
gebroðrum wistfullige on minum gebeorscipe." [12]

"John, come to me. It is time that with your brethren
you feast at my banquet."

Without knowing a word of Old English, a native speaker of today can understand a portion of this speech of God to John, whether he hears it read or reads the text himself. Little is lost in turning the passage into modern idiom although one may regret the passing of the compound "beer-ship," in the sense of "banquet," from the language. The more perfunctory annals in the *Saxon Chronicle* are likewise written in the simplest form. Thus, under the year 898 we read:

> Her on þysum gere gefor Æðelm Wiltun scire eal-
> dormon.[13]

> In this year Athelm Lord of Wiltshire died.

A considerable amount of Old English prose is on a relatively sophisticated level, however, especially that taken immediately from Latin writings, like the Alfredian translations of Boethius's *Consolation of Philosophy* and Bede's *Ecclesiastical History of the English People*. Apart from passages like that quoted above, Ælfric's sermons commonly reveal the grammatical and rhetorical influence of Latin. Again, when the writers of the *Chronicle* pause to deplore the evils of their times or to pass judgment about a ruler or archbishop, they too employ a larger vocabulary and more complex syntax. The shrewd appraisal of William the Conqueror appearing in one manuscript of the *Chronicle* provides an example:

> Gif hwa gewilnigeð to gewitane hu gedon mann he
> wæs oððe hwilcne wurðscipe he hæfde oððe hu fela
> lande he wære hlaford, þonne wille we be him awritan
> swa swa we hine ageaton ðe him on locadon & oðre
> hwile on his hirede wunedon. Se cyng Willelm þe we
> embe specað wæs swiðe wis man & swiðe rice, &
> wurðfulre and strengere þonne ænig his fore genga
> wære.[14]

If anyone wishes to know how accomplished a man he was or what honor he had or how many lands he was

ruler of, then we will write about him just as we per-
ceived him to be, we who have looked upon him and
at one time have dwelt in his household. The King
William of whom we speak was a very wise man and
very powerful and more worshipful and stronger than
any of his predecessors had been.

Even the nearly word-for-word version given above
may be considered acceptable Modern English. Only a few
expressions may not suitably and naturally be rendered by
their modern descendants, and the parallel structures of the
original are, by and large, still current today. At the same
time, the relatively free word order of the Old English is no
longer possible, and thus the intonation patterns of the author may not be exactly duplicated. One can conclude that
the process of translation does not seriously distort the total
effect achieved in Old English prose literature although it
behooves the user of translations, especially of the homilies
or the beautiful prefaces ascribed to King Alfred, to bear in
mind that he is not listening to the true accents of the
writers.

The language problems presented by Middle English
literature taken as a whole are less formidable than those of
Old English. The rapid disappearance of inflections on
nouns and adjectives, the loss of grammatical gender, and
the development of compensatory devices such as more
rigid word order and increased use of prepositions resulted
in a language a long step closer to that of modern times in
sentence structure and sound. One may not assume, however, that he can read all Middle English with only the aid
of a glossary, as he reads Chaucer. Considerable changes
took place in the centuries between 1100 and 1500. Moreover, in contrast to Old English literature, which happens
to have been written down for the most part in a single
dialect, that of Wessex, or the Channel coast area, Middle
English writings come down to us in several quite distinct
dialects. One may say that Middle English embraces in

effect a number of rather different languages and that each of them underwent changes peculiar to itself.

The regional forms of Middle English tend to differ from each other at least slightly in vocabulary, grammar, and pronunciation. In the North of England, for example, speakers used -s in present indicative plural verb forms, saying "they comes," "we raises," "the Scotsmen has taken," and the like. The present-day reader, then, must not be tempted to regard the author of the following passage from the poem *Pearl* as illiterate:

The yates stoken was never yet.[15]

The gates was never closed.

Elsewhere than in the North, standard usage decreed "the Scotsmen hath" or "the Scotsmen have" and "the gates weren" or "the gates were." Vocabulary peculiarities are exemplified especially by usages of the Northwest Midlands, where *dreely* in the sense of "continually" and *cadge* meaning "to bind" appear in poetry. Indeed, these expressions are said still to be heard in the Lancashire region. One should also be prepared to recognize spellings that are indicative of dialectal pronunciations. Thus, *vader* ("father") and *zenne* ("sin") are hallmarks of the speech of Kent. And the reader who remains innocent of the fact that *rape* and *stain* in Northern writings, such as the ballads, are likely to be the dialectal forms of "rope" and "stone" will fall into extraordinary difficulties. Clearly, without some awareness of these and other characteristics of Middle English, one can all too readily miss both the meaning and the word-music of the poetry of the period.

A general change that affected all Middle English dialects, although in varying degrees, was the augmentation of the Old English word stock by foreign borrowings, chiefly Norse and French. These vocabulary additions reflect, of course, two great historical movements—the Norse invasions and settlements in the ninth, tenth, and eleventh centuries, and the Norman Conquest of 1066 and the subsequent centuries of close association of England and parts of France. Besides affecting the vocabulary of English, the presence of Norse and then French speakers may also, although in ways not fully understood, have hastened the breakdown of inflections and brought about other changes in the language. The Norse vocabulary contributions, although much less numerous than the French, were nevertheless of great importance and they came ultimately to be current in areas of England other than the Danelaw, or the northern and eastern sections of the country occupied by the invaders. We look to Norse origins for common words like *wrong, law, husband, knife,* and *window,* and even for our pronominal forms *they, their,* and *them.* Beginning in the North of England, these Norse-influenced forms gradually replaced the Old English *hie, hiere,* and *hem.* By the mid-twelfth century, Anglo-Norman words had begun to infiltrate English literary usage in force, and a century later the rate of borrowing was still higher and remained at that level into the fifteenth century. Even before Chaucer's day, discourse without resort to French borrowings was almost as impossible as it is today. Of the 10,000 French words said to have been taken into Middle English, at least 75 per cent are still in use. As a result of later loans, as much as one-fourth of the vocabulary of current English is French.

From the standpoint of language, the end of the Old English period, then, is marked by the loss of inflections and of distinctions in grammatical gender. With a few exceptions which need not be specified here, the Old English vowel sounds were kept without serious change throughout the Middle English period. But, beginning in the fifteenth century and continuing for perhaps two hundred years, the so-called Great Vowel Shift revolutionized the sounding of the long or stressed vowels until the pronunciations of the present day were at last achieved. One may simplify the operation of the Great Vowel Shift, which sets off Middle from Early Modern English, by observing that each of the long vowels, for reasons that remain conjectural, came to be articulated in a new way—specifically, the pronunciation tended to be "raised" or formed in a higher position in the mouth. Thus, Old and Middle English *gos*, pronounced "gose," developed into *goose* and Middle English *cleene*, pronounced "clane," into *clean*. Old and Middle English stressed *i* and *u*, already pronounced high in the mouth, came each to be combined with another vowel, or "diphthongized," for the sake of variation; hence, early *ride*, pronounced "reed," evolved into *ride*, and *hus*, pronounced "hoos," into *house*. That the sounding of vowels was still in the process of change at the very end of the sixteenth century is apparent in some of Shakespeare's rimes. Thus, Rosaline, speaking of Berowne's lovesick heart, suggests that he cause it to be bled:

> Rosaline: Alack!   let it blood.
> Berowne: Would that do it good? [16]

It was many years before the differentiation between the vowel sounds in *blood* and *good* came to be fixed in Standard English.

The great irony in the history of English is that spelling was more or less normalized in the late fifteenth and the succeeding century, a period when vowel pronunciations were still in a state of transition. The fact that early printers chose, in general, to retain the old vowel symbols even for sometimes drastically shifted pronunciations explains to a large extent the disjunction between Modern English orthography and vowel sounds.

These few linguistic facts will help introduce the reader to the literary language, or languages, of Middle English times. To read the writings of the twelfth and even the early thirteenth centuries is not a great deal less difficult than to read Old English. But, with the vanishing of almost the last vestiges of case endings and other early features and with the absorption of numerous loan words, the language begins to assume more and more a familiar sound and appearance. At the same time, some of the best of medieval poetry was composed in the local dialect of the

Northwest Midlands, a form of English that Chaucer himself might have had trouble understanding. The Southeast
Midlands or London dialect used by Chaucer, it must be
remembered, formed the basis for the later literary standard; hence the ready intelligibility of Chaucer's writings to
modern readers. In this connection, it is interesting to note
the treatment by a recent editor of a collection of Middle
English lyrics dating from the thirteenth century and preserved in a variety of dialects. To render these poems more
readable, the editor has turned them into something approaching the language of Chaucer.[17]

The best of the earlier Middle English literature is
well represented by Layamon's *Brut,* composed possibly
as early as 1190 in the Southwest Midlands. The
poet speaks about the sources of his chronicle poem as
follows:

He nom þa Englisca boc,   þa makede seint Beda.
Anoþer he nom on Latin,   þe makede seinte Albin,
And þe feire Austin   þe fulluht brouhte hider in.
Boc he non þe þridde,   leide þer amidden,
þa makede a Frenchis clerc   Wace wes i-hoten, 20
þa wel couþe writen,   and he heo ȝef þare æðelen
Ælienor þe wes Henries quene,   þes heȝes kinges.[18]

He took the English book which Saint Bede wrote.
A second book he took in Latin which Saint Albin
    composed,
And the fair Augustine who brought baptism here.
He took the third book and laid it among (the others),
Which a French clerk who was named Wace wrote,
Who knew well how to write, and he gave it to the
    noble
Eleanor, who was queen of Henry the high king.

Much in Layamon's alliterative poem, in which rime is also
introduced, may be self-consciously archaic. Certainly the
word order is occasionally close to that of old English, as in
"who baptism brought hither in," l. 18; grammatical

gender is preserved in the feminine accusative pronoun *heo*, l. 21, the antecedent of which is *boc*, a feminine noun in Old English, and also in the feminine dative article *þare*, l. 21; and an inflected genitive phrase is used rather than a more modern prepositional construction in *þes heȝes kinges*, l. 22. Moreover, several old words occur here which are almost completely lost in literary usage before the close of the Middle English period: *nom*, "took," ll. 16, 17, and 19; *þe* and *þa*, "who" and "which," ll. 16, 17, etc.; *fulluht*, "baptism," l. 18; *i-hoten*, "named," l. 20; and *æðelen*, "noble," l. 21. Of course, a reader must further be able to identify *hider*, l. 18, as "hither," *ȝef*, l. 21, as "gave," *couþe*, l. 21, as "could," and *heȝes*, l. 22, as "high." Even so, the proportion of immediately recognizable words is probably somewhat higher than may be found in pre-Conquest poetry, a result in part at least of the disappearance of an exclusively poetic diction and of the kennings to which the old poets were addicted.

That all poetry of the first century and a half after the Norman Conquest was not so close to Old English as Layamon may be demonstrated by a few lines from the subtle and witty debate, *The Owl and the Nightingale*. Also written in the Southwest, this work is perhaps no later than 1200.

> Ich was in one sumere dale;
> In one suþe diȝele hale
> Iherde ich holde grete tale
> An Hule and one Niȝtingale.[19]

> I was in a summery valley;
> In a very secluded corner
> I heard holding a great debate
> An owl and a nightingale.

Aside from the old spellings *ich* for "I," first and third lines, and *hule* for "owl," fourth line, the principal difficulty the reader encounters is the phrase *in one suþe diȝele hale*, "in a very secluded corner," second line, containing three words common enough in Old English but of limited currency later. Once these words are understood, however, he can read the passage and perhaps catch the meaning from hearing it read aloud. An important reason for the fairly ready comprehensibility of this poem is that the syntax—the usual order of subject, verb, and modifiers—is more modern than Layamon's. Perhaps the rimed, metrical verse form of *The Owl and the Nightingale,* an innovation which Middle English poets seem to have taken over from the Latin and French, encouraged a less old-fashioned mode of expression than did a continuance of the ancient alliterative tradition.

Recordings of early Middle English poetry are less common than those devoted to the works of Chaucer, but some notion of its general effectiveness may be gained from competent readings or performances with musical settings of the famous "Cuckoo Song," composed in the South of England during the first half of the thirteenth century:

> Sumer is í-cumen in;
>   Lludé sing, cuccu!
> Growéþ sed, and blowéþ med,
>   And springþ þe wudé nu.[20]

> Summer is come.
>   Sing loudly, cuckoo.
> The seed sprouts, the meadow blossoms,
>   And the wood burgeons anew.

Although these lines offer difficulties to an uninitiated reader or listener, he should be able to sense the tone and mood of a nature song from words such as "summer," "sing," "cuckoo," "groweth," and the like. What one notices in particular about the sound of Middle English poetry like the "Cuckoo Song," or perhaps his own efforts to read aloud Layamon's *Brut* or *The Owl and the Nightingale,* is the great frequency with which unstressed syllables must for metrical purposes be pronounced at the end of words carrying no such weak endings in Modern English.

In the lines given above, these syllables, including the pre-verbal *i-* in *i-cumen,* are marked with acute accents. The texture of Middle English verse is to a considerable extent established by giving metrical value to many unstressed syllables. The result is that relatively few words are needed to make up a given number of metrical feet. The poetic line, then, tends to be less packed and the pace somewhat slower and more deliberate than is common in more recent poetry. One might note in passing that each of the four-stress lines of Shakespeare's "Cuckoo Song" at the very end of *Love's Labours Lost* consists of five or six words in contrast to the four words per line in the Middle English poem. Certainly some of the simple charm and unparalleled freshness of the early lyrics and also the richer elaboration to be found in Shakespeare may properly be ascribed to such linguistic features. The same factors make effective translation or modernization of the lyrics especially difficult.

Much Middle English poetry, including some of fairly early date, need not and should not be turned into Modern English. Unfamiliar words and puzzling constructions are usually rather few in number and may easily be glossed for the reader. Other works, of course, are far less intelligible in their original forms and are almost inevitably read in translation. These include not only the very early transitional works like Layamon's *Brut* but also those later poems composed in dialects rather far removed from the language of the Southeast Midlands.

The English of the Northwest Midlands, as already suggested, is strongly different from that of the London area, yet in that dialect and also in Northeastern English were written several of the most beautiful and illustrious of medieval poems, all of them during the fourteenth century, such as *Sir Gawain and the Green Knight, Pearl,* and the alliterative *Morte Arthure.* These and certain other writings, including *Piers Plowman* and *St. Erkenwald,* comprise what literary historians are accustomed to call the alliterative revival, in view of the fact that in poetic form they represent a continuance of Old English alliteration. The

opening lines of *Sir Gawain and the Green Knight* provide
a sufficient illustration of the Northwest Midland dialect in
more or less its pure state:

> Sithen the sege and the assaut was sesed at Troye,
> The borgh brittened and brent to brondes and askes,
> The tulk that the trammes of tresoun ther wroght
> Was tried for his tricherie, the trewest on erthe.
> Hit was Ennias the athel and his highe kynde   5
> That sithen depreced provinces, and patrounes bicome
> Welneghe of al the wele in the West Iles . . .[21]

> After the siege and the assault were over at Troy,
> The city demolished and burnt to brands and ashes,
> The man[a] who there brought about acts of treason
> Was noted for his treachery, the veriest example on
>   earth.
> It was Aeneas the noble and his exalted kin   5
> Who later subdued provinces and became the patrons
> Of virtually all the wealth of the West Isles[b] . . .

As comparison with the literal translation demonstrates,
the sentence structure and word order of the *Gawain*-poet
are reasonably modern. The vocabulary, on the other hand,
gives much difficulty. In the first place, the dialect is conservative in its retention of Old English words, like *athel*, l.
5, "noble," no longer common elsewhere in literary usage.
Second, it utilizes many Old Norse and Old French borrowings not much used in other dialects and unknown in
later English. The Norse word *tulk*, l. 3, "man," is an example. The Old French loans in the lines quoted above
include *trammes*, l. 3, "devices" or "acts," and *depreced*, l.
6, "subdued." Such an admixture of loans is characteristic
of the alliterative poetry of the Northwest and North. For
many lines written in the dialect of *Sir Gawain*, an accurate
translation which catches the alliterative style and other

[a] Antenor(?).
[b] Wight, the Isle of Man, and the Orkneys.

poetic features of the original is nearly as difficult as the translation of Old English poetry.

To the reader or listener today, the contrast in intelligibility between *Sir Gawain* and Chaucer's poetry is striking. Moreover, most contemporary writings in the other dialects such as the South or the North Midlands are likely to seem only slightly more alien than Chaucer. As a general rule, then, the later Middle English poetry, with exceptions already noted, is within the grasp of the student of English literature. The losses inevitably attendant upon translation are seldom justified by the few language problems that any single work normally presents.

That a highly serviceable and even an artistic prose was developed by Old English chroniclers, historians, Biblical translators, and writers of state papers has already been noted. It seems to have maintained a status analogous to that of a modern standard language throughout the reigns of the four Norman kings, that is, through 1154, but beginning with the accession of Henry II, the first of the Angevins, whose realm embraced approximately two-thirds of France as well as England, the official and literary use of English prose went into eclipse. The final entry in the *Saxon Chronicle* is 1154; all the evidence suggests that during the succeeding half-century, at least, English was not even a second language among the members of the ruling classes and that a knowledge of English did not become common in those social strata for perhaps two generations. The cultural prestige of France, the great numbers of peers of French family, and English preoccupation with French affairs were largely responsible, of course. That is, these cultural and social forces undermined the old prose tradition and effectively inhibited the rise of a new standard English for an astonishingly long period.

Norman French, in fact, came to be the medium of communication in court, grammar schools, and judicial processes, and it was widely used also in gild transactions and even much private correspondence. Beyond such utilitarian applications, an Anglo-Norman literature in prose and poetry, some of it composed in England proper, achieved a vogue. Besides numerous pious works, we have histories by Geffroi Gaimar and Wace, romances like *Tristan,* and a text of the *Chanson de Roland.* The writing of French literature for consumption in England continued at a diminishing rate until Henry of Lancaster's *Livre de Seyntz Medicines* (1354) and John Gower's *Mirour de l'Omme* (about 1380) strike us as outdated. Naturally, the native tongue in the several regional dialects remained the only language of the illiterate masses although this was the period when French borrowings began to filter into general use. It is not surprising that English persisted as a vehicle for literature only in religious writings addressed to the multitudes. Besides the very early "Cnut's Song," the poetry, like the *Moral Ode* (about 1170), that has come down to us dwells on religion. By the same token, the continuity of English prose through this period is maintained only in sermons and related works of moral exhortation.

The thirteenth century saw the tables turned in the competition between the two languages as the result of often-cited historical developments: first, the growth of national sentiment after King John's loss of Normandy in 1204; second, the success of King Philip Augustus in persuading many English noblemen possessing fiefs on both sides of the Channel to transfer their fealty to the French crown; and third, the outbreak of the Hundred Years' War. By 1200 and the immediately succeeding decades, English literature seems to have come to life again with the composition of poems like Layamon's *Brut* and the *Debate of the Body and the Soul* and also the major prose work, *Ancrene Riwle.* But whereas a variety of themes came soon to be exploited in verse, prose writing remained strangely confined to the field of religious and meditative works. Even in the fourteenth century, the several important prose works, except for the luminous discourses of the great mystics, seem to us somewhat unpracticed and awkward in execution, a stricture that applies as well to Chaucer's prose pieces.

Chief among prose writers contemporary with Chaucer are Thomas Usk, who wrote *The Testament of Love*; John Wyclif, who, with his followers, is responsible for sermons and tracts as well as the famous English Bible; and the author of the English form of *The Travels of Sir John Mandeville*. Despite these examples, resistance to the literary employment of English prose persisted. Translators of French prose works, such as the "Vulgate" version of the Arthurian romances, often resorted to English couplets in this period, and other writers maintained the tradition of composing perfectly commonplace manuals of instruction and history in verse. But the rapidly growing prestige of spoken English, as in courts of law and in the parsing of Latin lessons in grammar schools, made for a change in attitude. During the first half of the fifteenth century, the beginning of the Early Modern English period, English prose became established in literature. It is true that as late as the 1430's we find Henry Lovelich, a London gildsman, translating the *Merlin* and the *Holy Grail* from French prose into very bad English verse, but within a short time an anonymous rendering of much of this same material into relatively sound English prose made its appearance. Then came Malory's *Le Morte Darthur* and the less consistently effective writing in Caxton's translations and prefaces.

When we survey the whole tradition of Middle English prose, we are likely to feel that the earliest examples, such as the post-Conquest entries in the *Saxon Chronicle*, are only slightly less difficult than Old English. The twelfth-century clerics who continued the *Chronicle*, however, may have been influenced in the direction of archaic usage by the nature of their task. A fairer sample of early Middle English prose appears in *Ancrene Riwle*, a book of advice to religious recluses or ancresses. Composed probably in the closing years of the twelfth century, it was soon turned

from English into French and Latin. A frequently quoted
passage of this work reads as follows:

> ȝe, mines leove sustren, bute ȝef neod ow drive
> ant ower meistre hit reade, ne schulen habbe
> na beast bute cat ane. Ancre þe haveð ahte
> þuncheð bet husewif, ase Marthe wes.[22]

> You, my dear sisters, unless need drive you
> and your master counsel it, shall have
> no animal except for one cat. An ancress who has
>   property
> appears rather to be a housewife, as Martha was.

The Southwest Midlands dialect of this work retains many
old features. Among them is the pre-verbal position of some
direct objects, as in *ow*, "you," and *hit*, "it." Again, we find
a double negative in the first sentence quoted above, a
common enough tendency in Old English.

Ancrene Riwle is an important monument in the long
tradition of religious treatises in prose that continued into
the Renaissance. Chronologically arranged, these works
show a steady increase in suppleness of expression, and it
becomes all the more puzzling that prose was not more
widely utilized by other than religious or mystical writers.
The style of Richard Rolle, an early fourteenth-century
mystic, is especially fluent in the modern sense:

> Verray luf [a] clenses þe saule,[b] and delyvers it fra þe
> pyne[c] of hell, and of the foule servys of syn, and of þe
> ugly felyschip of þe devels; and of þe fendes sonn
> makes God sonn, and parcenel [d] of þe heritage of
> heven.[23]

Chaucer's prose, written nearly a half century later,
contains fewer unfamilar words than the writings of Richard Rolle, yet it is seldom as pleasing and natural to the
modern ear:

[a] love.   [b] soul.   [c] torment.   [d] partaker.

A yong man called Melibeus, myghty and riche, bigat upon his wyf, that called was Prudence, a doghter which that called was Sophie. Upon a day bifel that he for his desport is went into the feeldes[a] hym to pleye. Hys wyf and eek[b] his doghter hath he left inwith his hous, of which the dores were faste yshette.[24]

Chaucer's *Tale of Melibee*, his *Treatise on the Astrolabe*, and his *Boece*, or translation of Boethius's *Consolation of Philosophy*, represent a rather timid extension of prose beyond its usual limits. Not until the fifteenth century did prose come into its own in England in the fields of history, science, letters, and romance. Caxton printed a large amount of prose in the ninety-odd books that issued from his press, and none of these is more famous than his edition of Sir Thomas Malory's *Le Morte Darthur* (1485). In this great work, and in the writing of Pecock and Fortescue in the same century, English prose at last reached full maturity. That is, it became an artistic instrument of power and flexibility, as in such descriptions as this from *Le Morte Darthur*:

Than sir Bedwere departed and wente to the swerde and lyghtly toke hit up, and so he wente unto the watirs syde. And there he bounde the gyrdyll aboute the hyltis, and threwe the swerde as farre into the watir as he myght. And there cam an arme and an honde above the watir, and toke hit and cleyght [c] hit, and shoke hit thryse and braundysshed, and than vanysshed with the swerde into the watir.[25]

The prose we find in the Authorized Version of the Bible (1611), then, had long been a true literary medium and not the exclusive province of religious or mystical writers.

[a] fields.   [b] also.   [c] clasped.

FURTHER READINGS

Baugh, Albert C., A *History of the English Language*, New York: Appleton-Century-Crofts, 1957.

Brook, G. L., *English Dialects*, London: Andre Deutsch, 1963.

Brower, Reuben A., ed., *On Translation*, Cambridge, Mass.: Harvard University Press, 1959.

Chambers, R. W., *On the Continuity of English Prose*, Early English Text Society, CLXXXVI (1957).

Pilch, Herbert, *Layamons "Brut." Eine literarische Studie*, Anglistische Forschungen, 91 (1960).

Wrenn, C. L., "On the Continuity of English Poetry," *Anglia*, LXXVI (1958), 41-59.

RECORDINGS

Anglo-Saxon Poetry, Readings from, by Gretchen Paulus and Francis P. Magoun, Jr., Harvard Vocarium, L-7000-01.
[The selections read are from the following works: *Anglo-Saxon Gospels; Brunanburh; The Dream of the Rood; Maldon; The Wanderer; The Seafarer;* Cædmon's *Hymn;* Cynewulf's *Elene; Anglo-Saxon Riddles,* Nos. 28 and 47; *The Wife's Lament; Beowulf;* and *Judith.*]

Beowulf, Cædmon's Hymn, and Other Old English Poems, by J. B. Bessinger, Jr., Cædmon TC 1161.
[Selections from *Beowulf,* Cædmon's *Hymn, The Dream of the Rood, The Wanderer, The Battle of Brunanburh,* and *A Wife's Lament.*]

Chaucer and Beowulf, by J. C. Pope and Helge Kökeritz, Lexington 5505.
[Pope reads *Beowulf* selections and Kökeritz reads passages from Chaucers' *General Prologue, The Wife of Bath's Prologue, The Prioress's Tale,* and *Troilus and Criseyde.*]

Debate of the Body and the Soul, selections, by F. N. Robinson, Harvard Vocarium L-990.

One Thousand Years of English Pronunciation, by Helge Kökeritz, Lexington 7650, 7655.
[The Old English, Middle English, and Early Modern English passages included in this recording are from the following works: *Beowulf,* Ælfric's "Homily on the Assumption of St. John the Apostle," *The Anglo-Saxon Gospels* (Luke

7:2-9), the Wyclif-Purvey translation of the same verses, the same verses in the Authorized Version, "The Cuckoo Song," *Piers Plowman*, a Kentish tale of the fourteenth century, Chaucer's *Canterbury Tales*, Chaucer's *Troilus and Criseyde*, and Caxton's Preface to *Eneydos*.]

IV. Popular
Christian Doctrine

        To recover the teachings of the medieval Church which formed so vital a part of literary backgrounds is not the simple task that it might appear to be. Even though the people at large could be counted on for a grasp of no more than the most elementary dogmas, certain of the greatest Middle English writers reveal at least fleetingly and fragmentarily an acquaintance with patristic learning and the sophisticated philosophy and theology of the Scholastics. It becomes necessary, then, to trace here a few leading trends of the high intellectual life of the times and then to characterize the doctrine taught by the parish clergy, the latter with careful attention to the formulations actually used in popular treatises and in sermons.

        The centuries-long succession of great philosophers who addressed themselves to the abiding problems of religion is one of the miracles of the Middle Ages. No other faith in history is distinguished by so prolonged and luxuriant a burgeoning of speculation on the nature of God and man as may be found in the works of the early Greek and Latin apologists and of such later thinkers as St. Augustine, Boethius, Abelard, St. Anselm, Peter Lombard, Hugh of St. Victor, St. Bernard of Clairvaux, Robert Grosseteste, St. Albert the Great, Roger Bacon, St. Bonaventure, St.

Thomas Aquinas, William of Occam, and Duns Scotus. The momentous advancement of Christian thought by these and numerous others has led one of the most important of present-day scholars in the field, Etienne Gilson, to observe that it was Christianity that kept philosophy alive rather than the reverse.

Even if space permitted, to attempt here a close, technical exposition of medieval religious thought would be as irrelevant as it would be presumptuous, for true philosophical and theological ideas probably do not figure much more commonly in the vernacular literature of the Middle Ages than in that of any other period. It has been well said that the uses and judgments of ideas of this order in literature will always be quite different from the uses and judgments of the same ideas in philosophical discourse. That is, philosophical concepts, when used by a poet, function only to forward his specifically literary purposes.[1] At the same time, the reader of *Piers Plowman* is scarcely disadvantaged if he recognizes in the character Kind Wit a personification of the Law of Nature as discussed by Scholastic philosophers. Again, a rather broad knowledge of the Boethian formulation of free will and of simple and conditional necessity is required for an appreciation of a famous mock-heroic passage in Chaucer's *Nun's Priest's Tale*:

> But I ne kan nat bulte[a] it to the bren,[b]
> As kan[c] the hooly doctour Augustyn,
> Or Boece,[d] or the Bisshop Bradwardyn,
> Wheither that Goddes worthy forwityng[e]
> Streyneth[f] me nedely[g] for to doon a thyng,
> 'Nedely' clep I symple necessitee.[2]

Despite his playful tone, Chaucer obviously expected his audience at least to have heard about the philosophical concepts of simple and conditional necessity.

For the sake of alerting readers to the ideas of this sort most often reflected in literature, a highly generalized

---

[a] sift.   [b] bran.   [c] is able to do.   [d] Boethius.
[e] foreknowledge.   [f] constrains.   [g] necessarily.

treatment of Christian philosophy is called for here. It is appropriate to begin with St. Augustine (354-430), Bishop of Hippo in North Africa, for in his work is to be found not only the first full rationale of Christianity but also the foundation of medieval orthodoxy. St. Augustine's great achievement was the fruit of his long inner struggle with his own youthful enthusiasms and also of his later controversies with deviant sects like the Pelagians.

The Platonic conception of God as the principle of absolute being underlies Augustine's Christianity. Motivated by love, God created the universe, the angels, man, and all lowlier denizens of earth. Each earthly creature represents an amalgam of matter and form, the latter being the image of the divine idea which confers existence on the individual. Likewise a compound of matter and form, of body and soul, man can recognize the divinity in his soul as well as the omniscience of God when contemplating such of his own attributes as his urge to seek truth. From man's point of view, the whole of visible creation, in fact, serves as a means of understanding God, a function that is fundamental to the medieval attitude toward the universe and toward Scripture. Augustine stops short of the Platonic view that man is endowed with a ready-made set of innate ideas; rather, he considers that man's soul possesses basic tendencies that lead him to an apprehension of divine ideas in God. The impairment of these tendencies, a consequence of the fall of Adam, makes the grace of God essential for man if he is to be saved.

A second late Roman writer whose influence in limited areas came to rival that of Augustine was Boethius (480-525). C. S. Lewis has said that to acquire a taste for *The Consolation* of Boethius is "almost to become naturalised in the Middle Ages." [3] *The Consolation of Philosophy*, in fact, was a perennial source of wisdom; in England alone it was studied by Anglo-Saxon clerics, translated by King Alfred, translated again by Chaucer, and once more by Queen Elizabeth.

The Consolation, written in an ancient form in which

prose and poetry alternate, is a dialogue between the author, now enduring his fall from the favor of the Gothic
ruler of Rome, Theodoric, and his old "nurse," Lady Philosophy, who is materialized before him in his distress. In
discoursing on the mutability of the things of this world,
Lady Philosophy speaks in the person of Dame Fortune,
emphasizing that the wise man never assumes that the gifts
of fortune—beauty, health, prosperity, high rank—are his
to keep. Lady Philosophy also instructs Boethius about the
human will, which is free even though man must exist in a
world created and governed by an omniscient God. These
two apparently contradictory notions—that man has free
will and that God knows all and foreordains all—are recon-
ciled in traditional Platonic terms. The key concept is the
"simplicity" of God, who dwells beyond time and who, in
fact, created time as a prime feature of the universe. That
which to man and the creatures of earth is present, past, or
future, is to God all embodied in the single instant of his
creation. Hence, man's freedom of choice is not con-
strained, from his point of view, by the fact that God in his
omniscience knows how he will use his freedom. Boethius
offers a philosophical rather than a religious solace here,
even though all that he says is compatible with Christianity. *The Consolation* remained the *locus classicus* in the
Middle Ages for the Christian view both of fortune and of
free will, and it supplied in the quasi-divine instructress,
Lady Philosophy, the prototype of a whole host of allegorical teachers in medieval literature. In the next chapter, a
more detailed comment about the connections between
fortune and free will is provided.

The term "scholasticism," often used rather loosely,
designates in its restricted sense the philosophical and theological thought of the period 1100 to 1500. A large number
of the men who created the movement, especially those associated with the early universities, were deeply involved in
assimilating and adapting to their Christian philosophy
those logical works of Aristotle which had been recently
recovered from the Arabs. Another tendency of the School-

men was the employment of the expository method inaugu-
rated or at least popularized by Peter Lombard (c. 1100-
1164) in his *Four Books of Sentences*.[4] The method consists, first, of announcing a proposition or article of faith,
such as "on the unity of the Trinity," and, second, of citing Scripture and patristic commentary by way of authenti-
cating and sustaining the proposition. Scarcely more than a
compilation of dogma with a modicum of philosophical argument, Lombard's *Sentences* nevertheless came in time to
serve as a university textbook. A large number of theologians, including St. Thomas Aquinas, thought of their own
writings chiefly as commentaries on or expansions of "the
Master of Sentences." But in works such as Thomas's
Summa Theologica,[5] the discourse that follows the statement of the dogma or "question" is a highly sophisticated
analysis taking into account Scripture and the views pro
and con of the Fathers and of the "Philosopher," Aristotle.

Still a third characteristic of Scholastic thought is a
preoccupation with the ancient problem of universals. Very
broadly stated, this question is whether a general concept,
such as "manness" or "stoneness"—that is, the name of
any species or genus—refers to a "reality" that is superior
to the reality of an individual man, stone, or the like. The
Christianized Platonism espoused by St. Augustine leads
directly to an affirmative answer, the Realist position, inas-
much as the world of sense from this viewpoint is little
more than the shadow cast by the hierarchy of ideas in the
mind of God, the true reality. The contrary, or Nominalist
position, is to the effect that that "reality" resides only in
the individuals and that general ideas or universals are mere
names, "the sound of voices." Certain of Aristotle's logical
works, such as his *Categories*, were found to lend support
to the Nominalist cause because of the Philosopher's claim
that universals have no existence apart from the individuals
embodying them and also because for him secondary substance, or the perceivable qualities of any object, constitutes
the central point of logic. Despite innumerable fine-drawn
disputes, this issue assumed more than academic impor-

tance to Christians because of its bearing on such questions as how the Trinity may be rationally explained.

The confrontation of Augustinian Realism and the new Nominalism buttressed by Aristotle led to more than a century of disputation and also to a great many efforts at reconciliation. Even in the twelfth century, before the battle lines were fairly drawn, John of Salisbury (c. 1115-1180), the English humanist who became Bishop of Chartres, made reference to several different solutions of the problem of universals. The most celebrated reconciliation, of course, is that of St. Thomas Aquinas (1225-1274). According to the Thomist view, universals are abstractions which man formulates in order to understand the world, and thus they have no reality apart from individuals. In keeping with this standpoint, Thomas, in a debate held at the University of Paris in 1270 with John Peckham, later Archbishop of Canterbury, maintained the thesis that man's body is inseparably part and parcel of his being, whereas Peckham sustained the traditional Augustinian notion of man as a "soul using a body."

Thomas along with others gave emphasis to a further opinion already mentioned—namely, that the visible creation, or the "book of nature," and the revealed word of God in Scripture provide two different sources for man's knowledge of God. This distinction encouraged the view that what we accept on faith need not coincide altogether with what we know by reason. In other words, a disjunction between theology and philosophy came about. The Church was from the first hostile to this separation, attributing it to the influence of Averroes, the Arabic commentator on Aristotle. In 1270 and 1277, Bishop Tempier of Paris with the endorsement of the pope proscribed numerous doctrines on the grounds of Averroism, and especially because they seemed to involve the heresy of "double truth"—that is, the affirmation that there are separate "truths" of philosophy and of theology. Along with Siger of Brabant, Thomas came under the condemnation in part because of his refusal to believe that the world may be proved to have been created in time. A very different kind of book that has an important bearing on medieval romance, *The Art of Courtly Love* by Andreas Capellanus,[6] was condemned at the same time and for roughly parallel reasons.

The age of Scholasticism closed in a flurry of controversy among the various schools of thought, and it also witnessed the revival of Augustinianism.

Literary reflections of the more esoteric theological and philosophical concepts are not to be expected. On the other hand, that doctrinal ideas and some patristic learning occur in Old English poetry has been indicated in an earlier chapter. As is made clear in a treatment of allegory in a later section of this book, Middle English literature uses Scriptural lore very liberally. Moreover, some writers display a rather easy familiarity with certain concepts and the terminology of the philosophers. Chaucer's allusion to simple and conditional necessity in his *Nun's Priest's Tale,* cited above, is only one of many instances. To this may be added the Pardoner's whimsical use of "substance" and "accident," terms of formal logic, in his diatribe against gluttony:

> Thise cookes, how they stampe, and streyne, and
>   grynde,
> And turnen substaunce into accident,
> To fulfille all thy likerous talent! [a] [7]

In a more serious vein, Theseus in *The Knight's Tale* puts the story of Palamon and Arcite into cosmic perspective by musing on the great chain of being, or love, and on the divine governance of the world, using the Aristotelian term "Prime Mover" for "God":

> The Firste Moevere of the cause above,
> Whan he first made the faire chayne of love,
> Greet was th' effect,[b] and heigh[c] was his entente.[d]
> Wel wiste[e] he why, and what therof he mente

[a] gluttonous desire.   [b] result.   [c] noble.   [d] purpose.
[e] knew.

For with that faire cheyne of love he bond
The fyr,[f] the eyr,[f] the water,[f] and the lond [f]
In certeyn bondes, that they may nat flee.[g] [8]

Numerous other ideas first formulated by the Fathers and by Scholastic philosophers find their way into Chaucer's works and they are not lacking in the other more learned poets of the age.

A very different strain of religious life in the later Middle Ages also left its mark on English literature—namely, speculative mysticism. The founders of this movement, including Denis (or Dionysius) the Areopagite (fifth or early sixth century) and St. Bernard of Clairvaux (1096-1141), proceed from the principle that God in his infinity is totally beyond the human intellect. Nevertheless, through the discipline of humility, compassion, and, finally, utter surrender to contemplation, one may rise to a sense of participation or union with God. The true quality of this experience is incommunicable, yet the mystic is able to describe the various stages of the "way," and, by analogy to sensory experiences such as sweetness, warmth, and joy, convey after a fashion the nature of the inner goal he seeks.[9] Mysticism produced a school of remarkable devotional writers in England, including Richard Rolle, Walter Hilton, and Dame Julian of Norwich, whose moving works in modernized form are kept in print to this day.

The fourteenth-century English mystics tended to draw their inspiration directly from the basic Latin works of their great exemplars. The anonymous *Deonise Hid Diuinite* ("Dionysius' Hidden Divinity"), for example, is a version of Dionysius's *De Mystica*, and another English treatise is taken from Richard of St. Victor. But the Middle English writers working outside the mystical tradition, including Chaucer, seem by and large to have derived their theological and doctrinal learning from second-hand sources, many of them in the vernacular. These English literary men, of course, were addressing

[f] (the four elements.)   [g] escape.

themselves to a broader, less sophisticated audience than the mystics had in view.

As suggested in the preceding chapter, the manuals prepared for priests and the numerous penitential and devotional treatises designed for the laity provide an excellent digest of parish doctrine. But in the medieval encyclopedias we have summaries of a more or less popular nature on a great variety of subjects. Isidore of Seville (c. 570-636), who abstracted a large amount of ancient wisdom in his *Origines* or *Etymologies*, seems to have established the tradition of encyclopedic writing. Perhaps the most learned and voluminous of his followers was Vincent de Beauvais (d. 1264), whose *Speculum Mundi* falls into separate treatises on natural history, Christian doctrine, and the like. In England, the chief encyclopedists were Alexander Neckam (1157-1217), whose *De Naturis Rerum* and *De Laudibus Divinae Sapientiae* discuss and criticize the learning and the centers of learning of his day, and Bartholomeus Anglicus (fl. 1250), whose *De Proprietatibus Rerum* covers a great range of knowledge. The considerable and long-lived vogue of Bartholomeus is demonstrated by the fact that his work was translated into English by John Trevisa in 1398, printed by Wynkyn de Worde in 1491, and used liberally by Jonson, Marlowe, and other Renaissance writers.

The encyclopedias, besides treating sacred matters, tend to follow a plan of organization based on the four elements. Thus, Bartholomeus's main topics are as follows: God, angels, the soul, the heavens, time, matter, form, fire, air (including the denizens of air, such as the birds), water (including the fish), and earth (including the regions of the earth, plants, animals, and the like).[10] This work, like its predecessors, carries over much quaint lore from the *Physiologus*, a very early and naïve work of Christian instruction having to do with the edifying properties of beasts, birds, herbs, and stones.[11]

The encyclopedias are of great value in helping us assess the kind of knowledge generally available, but here the interest is primarily in the penitential treatises, some of which draw upon the encyclopedists' summaries of astronomy, astrology, the doctrine of the four elements and the humors of the body, the ages of man, and other quasi-scientific material. The numerous *summae* of parochial theology fall into several categories. One group, based on the influential *Speculum Ecclesiae* of St. Edmund, Archbishop of Canterbury (d. 1240), provides commentaries on the seven sins, the seven virtues, the seven beatitudes, the seven petitions of the Lord's Prayer, the ten commandments, and the like. Besides French and English translations of the original Latin work, there is a free English adaptation. A second group stems from William of Wadington's *Manuel des Péchés*. Of this work, Robert Mannyng's *Handlyng Synne*, quoted in the Introduction, is a translation and expansion. Again, *The Ayenbite of Inwyt*, the somewhat later *Book of Vices and Virtues*, Chaucer's *Parson's Tale*, and Gower's *Mirour de l'Omme* are all derivatives in some way of the French *Somme le Roi*, written in 1279 by the Dominican Friar Lorens. Still other treatises exploit certain stereotypes of allegory, such as the *Livre de Seyntz Medicines* and *The Desert of Religion*.[12]

Religious works of this general sort became so numerous by the fifteenth century that one writer was prompted to remark:

> þer beþ so manye bokes & tretees of vyces and vertues & of dyuerse doctrynes, þat þis schort lyfe schalle raþere haue anende of anye manne þanne he maye owþere studye hem or rede hem.[13]

Their composers seem often to speak as though addressing layfolk, but there is reason to believe that their "lewd" readers included clergy as well. That is, many of the compendia probably served parish priests in good stead as handbooks of pastoral theology just as they served the restricted body of laymen able to read as aids in private devotions and in preparation for confession. As indicated earlier, the literate layfolk, whose pious interests helped create the demand for vernacular treatises, consisted mainly of the mercantile class in towns and perhaps a small number of gentry as well.

In the preceding chapters something has been said about the canonical obligations laid on the parish priest to instruct and admonish his parishioners in sermons and in confession. It would seem that in carrying out these duties, the clergy must often have relied not only on the English works just mentioned but also on manuals prepared expressly for their use, such as John Myrc's *Manuale Sacerdotis,* the same writer's English book, *Instructions for Parish Priests,* and Archbishop Thoresby's so-called *Lay Folks' Catechism.* The penitential treatises, the priests' manuals, and the sermons taken together furnish a fairly clear outline of the kind of Christian knowledge assimilated by the people and even of the verbal formulations in which such instruction was received.

To begin with, this religious literature gives primary emphasis to doctrinal matters which, in accordance with the decrees of Church councils and the directives or "constitutions" of bishops, every Christian was to know. At the very least, the Christian in Old English times, as later, was to know the Pater Noster, Hail Mary, and the Apostle's Creed, all in English, of course. If in confession he proved unable to recite all three to his confessor, he was theoretically to be given the penance of learning them. Moreover, the priest was ordered to preach several times each year on these rudiments of faith. Literature abounds with allusions to the "Pater," "Hail Mary," and the "Creed," sometimes in the course of noting that a child was too young to have memorized them or that parents or godparents were negligent in their duty. In the great fourteenth-century poem *Pearl,* the Dreamer remarks that the Pearl-maiden, who seems to have died at the age of two, knew neither Pater Noster nor Creed. Again, the seven-year-old "clergeon" in Chaucer's *Prioress's Tale* learned his "Ave Maria" from his mother. From all indications, the priest, in discoursing on the Pater Noster, commonly spoke of the seven petitions contained in the prayer. In "hallowed be thy name," we pray for the gift of wisdom; in "thy kingdom come," we pray for an understanding of our faults; in "thy will be done," we pray for good counsel; in "give us this day our daily bread," we pray for the everlasting bread of the altar; and so on.

The "Hail Mary" was sometimes taught in a rimed form, to judge from Myrc's *Instructions*:

> Hayl be þow mary fulle of grace;
> God ys wyþ þe in euery place;
> I-blessed be þow of alle wymmen,
> And þe fruyt of þy wombe Ihesus! Amen [14]

The rimed form of the Apostles' Creed given in the same work may represent closely what many Englishmen were taught. The opening lines read as follows:

> I beleue in oure holy dryȝt,[a]
> Fader of heuene god, almyȝt,
> þat alle thynge has wroȝt,
> Heuene and erþe & alle of noȝt:
> On ihesu cryst I beleue also,
> Hys only sone, and no mo,
> þat was conceyued of þe holy spyryt,
> And of a mayde[b] I-bore quyt.[b]
> And afterward vnder pounce pylate[c]
> Was I-take for vye[d] and hate,
> And soffrede peyne and passyone,
> And on þe croys was I-done.[e] [15]

In expounding the Creed either privately in confession or in a sermon, the priest apparently broke it down into a series of "articles of faith," twelve or fourteen in number. John Gaytryge's sermon (c. 1375), which is a translation of Archbishop Thoresby's *Catechism*, expands the treatment of the Creed with the statement that seven articles pertain

[a] lord. [b] complete maid (virgin). [c] Pontius Pilate.
[d] envy. [e] put to death.

to the Godhead, such as the first, "to believe steadfastly in a true God," whereas the other seven concern Christ's manhood, like the fourteenth, "just as he died and afterwards ascended into heaven, so shall he come to judge both the quick and the dead." [16] The central doctrine of the Creed, the Trinity, is the subject of many medieval sermons. Very often, in these the triune God is likened to identical reflections in the several fragments of a broken mirror or to the identical composition of water, snow, and ice.

Other Christian concepts and formulations were also recommended. Thoresby's *Catechism*, based to some extent on Peckham's *Constitutions* of the preceding century, urges the clergy to preach Sunday sermons on the following six fundamentals and furthermore to inquire in confession whether they were understood by the people: (1) the fourteen articles of the Creed, (2) the Ten Commandments of the law and the two of the gospel, (3) the seven sacraments, (4) the seven works of bodily and the seven of spiritual mercy, (5) the seven Christian virtues, and (6) the seven deadly sins. To this, the so-called Wycliffite version adds a note to the effect that the people should be warned against the sins entering the soul through the five senses.[17] The treatment accorded only a few of these points of doctrine may be reviewed here—namely, the Ten Commandments, the vices and virtues, and the sacraments of Eucharist and penance.

As would be expected, the Ten Commandments were constantly invoked in all forms of moral suasion. They were dealt with in countless sermons, they were a primary concern of the authors of the doctrinal tracts, and they must have figured prominently in the relentless interrogation of the penitent. Through such indoctrination, the medieval Christian could not fail to become thoroughly grounded in the anatomy of sin in all its ramifications. In connection with the first commandment, "I am the Lord thy God; Thou shalt have none other Gods but me," the priest was to make clear that this law condemns witchcraft, sorcery, love philters, and the like. The third commandment, "Thou shalt not take the Name of the Lord thy God in vain," is applied both to giving false testimony in the hall-mote and to the profanity of swearing by God's bones, heart, wounds, or nails. In explicating the fourth commandment, "Remember that thou keep holy the Sabbath-Day," the priest was to warn against shooting, wrestling, singing, and rioting on Sunday, especially at time of Mass. The fifth, "Honour thy father and thy mother," is extended to priests and other clerics. The tales used to illustrate each of the commandments in collections like Robert Mannyng's *Handlyng Synne* must have been freely borrowed for sermon composition.

The moralists were much interested in extending their exhortations to righteous conduct by presenting minutely detailed and lavishly allegorized treatments of the seven sins. The sermon of Chaucer's Parson and the "Confession of the Seven Deadly Sins" in *Piers Plowman* are completely traditional reflections of one of the most intense preoccupations of popular Christianity. In *The Ayenbite of Inwyt*, or "Remorse of Conscience," of about 1340, the supporting allegory involves a hideous seven-headed, many-horned beast which St. John sees emerging from the sea. Each head represents one of the sins, and subspecies are symbolized by the horns. Thus, the first head is pride, the beginning of all sin, since it was first committed by Lucifer in heaven. Pride is the devil's daughter, the king of wicked customs, and the lion that devours all. The seven horns or branches of pride are untruth, despite or scorn, arrogance, foul desire, vanity, hypocrisy, and foolish fear. Each of the horns in turn sprouts several twigs. Arrogance is subdivided into refusing to do as others do, the foolish spending of money to gain praise, false strife to support a wrong, boasting, scorn, and heedlessness to advice. In talking about vanity, the author seizes the opportunity to discourse in Boethian terms about the goods of nature, such as health, beauty, strength, and good understanding; the goods of fortune, such as rank or riches; and the goods of grace, or virtue and good works. A stern warning is issued to fools who would be beguiled by Dame Fortune and her false wheel, and the argument continues to liken the goods of fortune to the twelve winds of idle bliss which lull man into doting on physical comfort, luxury, lustful behavior, and worldly dignity.

The other six heads of the beast, of course, are envy, wrath, sloth, avarice, lechery, and gluttony, each of which is analyzed in much the same way as pride. Envy is said to be the adder which poisons the heart and leads to sins against the Holy Ghost, such as despair of salvation. Hate is manifested in the man who despises both others and himself. Sloth is the disinclination to do good when it should be done, such as attendance at Mass. Avarice conduces not only to theft, usury, and stinginess, but even to sacrilege, such as stealing from the Church by withholding tithes. Lechery includes fornication, adultery, incest, and unnatural sexual practices. Gluttony is broadly interpreted to cover not merely immoderate eating and drinking, by which man makes a god of his belly, but also sins of the tongue, or evil speech and blasphemy.[18] Some moralists speak about the eating of the fruit in the Garden as an act of gluttony or even of avarice. Still others display a fondness for referring to the tavern as the devil's chapel in which a travesty on Christ's miracles is to be seen in the transformation produced by drunkenness, a notion beautifully illustrated in *Piers Plowman*.

In other treatises, the seven sins are figured as animals. In particular, the moralists speak not only of the lion of pride and the serpent of envy, as does the author of *Ayenbite of Inwyt*, but also of the unicorn of wrath, the bear of sloth, the fox of avarice, the sow of gluttony, and the scorpion of lechery. Occasionally these animal associations appear in literary works. One especially ingenious tract, *Jacob's Well*, likens the sins to seven different layers of mud or ooze which befoul the pit of lust, or man's body. The pit may be cleansed only by dipping out the filth with the ladle of penance.[19] In numerous treatises the sins take the form

of soldiers who, under the captaincy of the devil, assault
man's body, his castle, in an effort to reach the soul. Such
allegories involve also the concept of the five outer wits or
bodily senses, thought of as gateways to sin. The gates must
be guarded most diligently if the soul is to be saved. An
Anglo-Norman treatise, Henry of Lancaster's *Livre de
Seyntz Medicines*, written in 1354 by Henry, first Duke of
Lancaster and one of the greatest men of Edward III's day,
combines the imagery of the five gateways of the castle
with the long-established tendency to speak of sins as dis-
eases or lesions of the body and the sacraments and teachings of the Church as holy poultices and remedies. In
Henry's relentlessly complete allegory, each of the five
senses or gateways to the soul is weakened by the effects of
sin. The diseased mouth, for example, produces a suppura-
tion representing the whole rout of deadly sins. To the
wounded senses, the Christian must apply such remedies as
the milk or tears of the Blessed Virgin or the Blood of
Christ. Finally, the diseased gateways must be bandaged
with the linen of the Trinity if the infectious air of tempta-
tion is to be excluded.[20] This allegory in which certain
virtues are recommended as "remedies" for deadly sins is
also reflected in Chaucer's *Parson's Tale*.

By far the most common device used by writers,
preachers, and even artists, however, is the tree figure. In
the moral tracts, again including *The Parson's Tale*, the
sections dealing with the sins and virtues make liberal use
of imagery connected with the basic notion of a tree, such
as "branch," "twig," and "leaf." *The Ayenbite of Inwyt*
and another treatise called *The Desert of Religion* present
forested landscapes, including not only trees of vices and
virtues, but trees of humility, of worldly vanity, of the sacraments, of chastity, of perfection, of mercy, and the like.[21]
Drawings of the trees of vices and virtues are to be found in
manuscripts of moral tracts and also, as noted earlier, on
the walls of churches. Usually appearing in pairs, the trees
of vices and virtues are similarly drawn, consisting of a
trunk growing out of a pot with three leafy branches sym-

metrically arranged one on each side. The tip of the tree of vices, also bearing leaves, is labeled *luxuria,* or lechery, and the three branches on either side of the trunk bear the Latin names of the other sins. Since the pot holding the tree is designated *superbia,* or pride, always recognized as the chief of the deadly sins, pride appears again as one of the branches, although there it is usually given the alternate name of vainglory. The seven or more leaves on each branch and the tip represent a bewildering series of subdivisions of each of the sins. Hanging from the limb vainglory, for example, are hypocrisy, disobedience, presumption, arrogance, recklessness, pertinacity, and loquacity. Lechery displays such subdivisions as voluptuousness, libido, fornication, and the like. The species of the sins vary from one drawing or treatise to another; moreover, the graphic representations differ a good deal in their degree of elaboration. Some of them show such additional features as pictures of a king or Dives and the Old Adam.

Other pictorial and carved representations of the seven sins include a wheel of sins and conventionalized personifications, such as are described in the well-known "Confession of the Deadly Sins" in *Piers Plowman.* All the visual aids aim at teaching the classical Christian theory of sin— namely, that sinful conduct of all kinds is at last the result of the individual's pride or self-love, of his placing his own physical ease and self-esteem above love of God and neighbor. As the product of one basic defect, the seven conventionally distinguished sins are organically related to each other.

The tree of virtues is intended to illustrate quite as forcefully the interrelatedness of temperance, fortitude, prudence, justice, faith, hope, and charity. The first four are the so-called cardinal virtues, stemming from classical writers, and the last three are the theological virtues. The tip of the tree is charity, or the perfect love of God, and the two topmost branches, faith and hope. The remaining branches represent the cardinal virtues, and the pot at the base is labeled humility—that is, self-abasement. The leaves symbolize subspecies, just as they do in the tree of sins. For example, fortitude is decorated with leaves called stability, constancy, tolerance, confidence, and the like. Charity at the top is surrounded by foliage standing for qualities like piety, grace, peace, and mercy. Pictures of God, angels, and the New Adam or Christ are sometimes set in medallions along the trunk or in the margins. The beholder could scarcely fail to meditate on how the virtues all flow from humility, the antithesis or "remedy" of pride.

The wheel device was also used for graphic illustration of the means of salvation. In a manuscript copy of a priests' manual, for example, a wheel with seven concentric circles inside it is depicted, the innermost circle representing the petitions of the Pater Noster, the second the sacraments, the third the gifts of the Holy Ghost, and so on.[22]

The seven sacraments—baptism, confirmation, Eucharist, penance, matrimony, orders, and unction—are dealt with in virtually all the doctrinal tracts and in numerous sermons. William of Shoreham, a Kentishman of the early fourteenth century, for example, has left us a clear and informative treatise on the sacraments in a series of poems.[23] Most of the tracts and sermons, it should be noted, are concerned with the externals of the sacraments, "the outward and visible signs," rather than with theory.

Thus, expositions of the Eucharist, or the Mass, dwell chiefly on conduct in church and the taking of communion. The people seem to have been regularly exhorted to leave off speech and jesting upon entering the church, and they were not to lean against the wall or a pillar but rather to "sit on their knees" on the floor except when standing, as at the reading of the Gospel. During the Mass, no responses were expected, but the parishioner was urged to repeat silently the Pater Noster and Ave over and over while the priest intoned in an unknown tongue. During the reading of the Mass Creed, the Nicene, he was to frame the words of the Apostle's Creed in his mind. *The Layfolk's Massbook*, translated late in the Middle Ages from the French, provides a full set of prayers and devotional meditations for the Mass, although the Latin liturgy is by no means actually translated except for the "Gloria," the Pater Noster, and one or two other prayers and responses. Obviously intended for people literate in English but unable to follow the Latin of the service, this prayer book was most used, it appears, by gentry and merchants. Its general nature may be illustrated by the procedure recommended at the Offertory. The parishioner was instructed either to stay in his place or to go forward with his Mass penny after the reading of the Creed. Whichever he did he was to say a one-sentence prayer silently, petitioning Christ to fulfill good desires. Thereafter, during the washing of hands, he was to repeat his Pater Noster to himself. Somewhat similar advice is given for each step in the Canon of the Mass. *The Prymer or Lay Folks' Prayer Book* provided another set of private devotions, including the Hours of the Blessed Virgin, to be read by the parishioner during the church service.[24]

The purpose of such works as John Lydgate's *Merits of the Mass* was likewise to lead "the lewd who cannot understand Latin" into proper thoughts before and during Mass. At the ringing of the sanctus bell, Lydgate tells the Christian, he must pray for sufficient worthiness to behold the consecration; at the fraction of the Host, he should think about the sorrow and torment endured by Christ; and at the priest's communion, he should pray to the Holy Ghost that he might also be "housled." [25] Upon receiving communion himself, usually only at Easter, the layman is warned against chewing the Host too fine lest fragments should be embedded in his teeth. The very nature of the Eucharist invited the medieval layman, with his rich heritage of folk beliefs, to invest the sacrament with an aura of magic. It has already been noted how laypeople in towns sometimes rushed from one church to another in order to witness several consecrations and thus multiply their spiritual benefits. Tales involving the transmutation of the consecrated wafer into a living child or the risen Christ were popular. Such a Eucharistic miracle, in fact, marks the great culmination of the Grail quest legend.

One of John Myrc's sermons repeats the old notions that a Christian will not die a sudden death on the day that he communicates and that he will not grow older during the celebration of Mass. In the same sermon appears an exemplum concerning St. Ode, Archbishop of Canterbury, who, in rebuking skeptical clerics, demonstrated that blood runs into the chalice upon the fraction of the Mass wafer.[26]

The reasons for the heavy stress placed on the sacrament of penance beginning early in the thirteenth century have already been treated. It has been noted that the new obligation laid on every Christian to confess at least once annually was largely responsible for the development of a rather systematic instructional program, expressed in official pronouncements of the Church, a variety of writings intended for priests and laity, and sermons. The most important aim of the instruction was to prepare the layman for confession by reminding him of his sinfulness. It is not surprising, then, that expositions of penance occupy a central place in all popular teachings. Beyond making clear what the Christian must know in order to lead a righteous life, the moralists dwell on the three parts of the sacrament —confession of the mouth, or "open shrift of the mouth how we sinned"; contrition of the heart, or "sorrow in heart that we have sinned"; and satisfaction, or "rightwys amends-making of sins." The confessor was admonished to assist in the making of a full and open confession, not "wrapped in silk," by interrogating the penitent about his involvement in the cardinal sins and the sins of the five wits and also about his understanding of standard dogmas. The principal sign of contrition, or true sorrow for sin, was the penitent's "low heart and weeping eyes." Only with some assurance that sorrow was present could the priest properly pronounce absolution. The satisfaction or penance meted out was likely to consist of prayers, fasting, or almsdeeds, and the sinner was solemnly enjoined to perform it. Penance in later medieval times was probably somewhat more severe than is common today, yet it was far slighter, it would appear, than the terms imposed in the Old English period when confession was a less regular practice and when the old penitential handbooks were widely used. The Christian was given to understand that if he did too little penance on earth, his term in purgatory would be correspondingly longer.

A few other aspects of penance were taught as well, such as the list of grievous sins, like sodomy, reserved for the bishop's absolution. The priest was constantly reminded about the sacrosanct nature of confession secrets. Only occasionally does a treatise, like *The Pricke of Conscience*, allude to the general theory underlying penance and indulgences—namely, the concept of the treasury of grace stored up by the merits of Christ and the saints to which the Church holds the keys. It is by drawing upon this treasury that the priest is able to absolve the penitent, "to loose or bind," in the words of the Bible (Matt. 16:19).[27] Some writers speak of the "graces of confession," which include such formulas as "shrift injures the fiend of hell," "shrift is God's messenger," and "shrift is the gate of heaven."

Numerous other doctrinal and devotional matters are covered in popular Christian instruction. Some treatises and occasional sermons, for example, touch on the religious view of the physical universe, a subject reserved for the next chapter. Beyond this, one finds discourses on sacrilege, the great sentence of excommunication, fortune, the fourteen pains of hell, the pains of purgatory, the joys of heaven, the five wounds of Christ, the seven gifts of the Holy Ghost, the five joys of the Virgin Mary, and exhortations entitled "how to know good and evil" and "learn how to die well." Middle English writers, and especially the authors of the lyrics, made frequent use of these devotional formulations.

Because the Bible was "the most studied book of the Middle Ages," [28] it is surprising that the teaching of Scripture as such is not explicitly included in the program of

Christian knowledge to be imparted to the laity. The great scarcity of Bibles throughout the age may be one explanation. At the same time, many sermons were preached on the propers from Scripture, and much incidental Biblical material is quoted or paraphrased in the treatises. John Myrc has left us a sermon for the fourth Sunday in Lent explicating the parable of the loaves and the fishes (John 6:1), the gospel for the day. The first three of the five loaves, according to Myrc, represent the three parts of penance and the remaining two are meant to remind the Christian to fear returning to sin and to persevere in virtue. The two fish stand for the two general categories of penitential acts—prayer and almsgiving.[29]

One of the widely used tracts—*Cursor Mundi*, or "Overrunner of the World"—stands out from the rest by reason of its effort to convey to readers no small part of Biblical history. This early fourteenth-century English work, based on a twelfth-century synopsis by Peter Comestor and containing echoes of the apocryphal *Gospel of Nicodemus*, is organized according to the seven ages of the world: (1) the Trinity and the creation; (2) the flood; (3) the age of Abraham; (4) the age of King David; (5) the birth of Christ; (6) the baptism of Christ by John the Baptist; and (7) Anti-Christ and doom. Intimations of the Christian dispensation are worked into the Old Testament portions of the story, and much of the standard instructional program is incorporated in the two final sections. Such a work must have been of considerable value for the medieval preacher. Portions of *Cursor Mundi* are reminiscent of the much later mystery plays, especially those concerning Old Testament history.[30]

FURTHER READINGS

Bloomfield, Morton W., *The Seven Deadly Sins*, Lansing: Michigan State College Press, 1952.

Dawson, Christopher, *Religion and the Rise of Western Culture*, London: Sheed and Ward, 1950.

Gilson, Etienne, *History of Christian Philosophy in the Middle Ages*, New York: Random House, 1955.

Holmes, Urban Tigner, Jr., *Daily Living in the Twelfth Century, Based on the Observations of Alexander Neckam in London and Paris*, Madison: University of Wisconsin Press, 1952.

Katzenellenbogen, Adolf, *Allegories of the Virtues and Vices in Mediaeval Art*, New York: W. W. Norton and Co., 1964.

Pepler, Conrad, *The English Religious Heritage*, St. Louis, Mo.: B. Herder Book Co., 1958.

Pieper, Josef, *Scholasticism: Personalities and Problems of Medieval Philosophy*, New York: Pantheon Books, 1960.

V. The World View
of the Middle Ages

A product of Greek culture, the geocentric conception of the visible universe was systematized by Aristotle, mathematically refined by Ptolemy, and further elaborated by the Arabs. It was this cosmology rather than that of the Pythagoreans, proponents of which taught that the earth revolves about the sun, that chanced to survive most vigorously into the Middle Ages. In eighth-century England, Bede was able to acquire a good knowledge of the Ptolemaic system, including an understanding of the rotundity of the earth and the order of the enveloping spheres of the planets. Another work testifying to the prevalence of such knowledge in Old English times is the *Handboc* of Byrhtferth, a late tenth-century monk. This curious manual, written in both Latin and English, deals not only with astronomical concepts but also with mathematics, verse-craft, and the vices and virtues.[1]

The world system which placed the earth at the center of a nest of marvelously rotating spheres carrying on their surface the heavenly bodies was never formally a part of the program of Christian education discussed in the preceding chapter. Nevertheless, because it was implicit in all that was said and written about God's creation, the Ptolemaic universe must in its general outlines have been understood and accepted as literal truth by medieval Christians just as today the very different solar system may be said to be at least dimly and crudely apprehended by people without the benefit of astronomical learning. Perhaps C. S. Lewis is right in holding that "ditchers and alewives" were in ignorance about the "model" of the medieval universe,[2] yet even these humble and illiterate people must have been given some exposure to the system by their parish priests. Philosophers, encyclopedists, and moralists were all intent on demonstrating the hand of God in every aspect of his creation with the result that the accepted cosmology in the most technical details of its busy machinery came to serve the purposes of religion to a degree probably unparalleled in the history of thought. Of course, the entire pageant of the heavens—the fixed stars twinkling on the distant celestial sphere and the seven planets wheeling grandly along the zodiacal path—provided in itself testimony to the perfection of God's order. The most impressive efforts of the philosophers were devoted to perceiving the divinely established analogies or links between the heavens and the purposes of God so far as man is concerned. In developing these links, they utilized with eclectic ingenuity much ancient lore and several concepts from late Greek thought.[3] Most important among these fragments from the pagan past were the doctrine of the four elements, astrological and numerological superstitions, the notion of the goddess Fortuna, and miscellaneous Platonic and neo-Platonic concepts having to do with the triad, the nine orders of angels, and the great chain of being. The result—the vast, comprehensive rationale of God's Providence or governance of the universe uniting in seamless unity the physical and moral realms—was perhaps the most sublime achievement of the medieval mind.

The cosmology, the skeleton supporting the vast hierarchy of creation, came itself to be highly elaborated by medieval astronomers. The sophistication of these scientists is reflected in general works like St. Thomas Aquinas's commentary on the astronomy of Aristotle and Vincent of

Beauvais' mid-thirteenth-century encyclopedia, *Speculum Naturale*. More austerely mathematical are the treatises and astronomical tables of John of Linnières and Thomas of Wallingford in the fourteenth century. Without telescopes or chronometers, such men were able to predict the courses of the planets and plot the stars with astonishing accuracy. Their only instruments were cumbersome geometrico-mechanical devices like the astrolabe and the equatory of the planets. Chaucer, it will be recalled, wrote *A Treatise on the Astrolabe*, dedicating it to his son, "lite Lowys." [4] Another late fourteenth-century work, which deals with the equatory of the planets and includes mathematical computations, is accepted by some as also the work of Chaucer.[5]

Medieval literature is saturated with allusions to the old cosmology and to the ways in which it manifests the purposes of God. Astrological influences are also very frequently represented, sometimes by way of illustrating the whims of fortune. In Chaucer's *Knight's Tale*, for example, the fortunes of Palamon and Arcite and character motivation in general are made heavily dependent on the planets, or rather the quarrels and bickerings among the pagan gods whose names the planets bear. Dante's *Divine Comedy*, of course, offers the classical instance of a great work utilizing to the full the moral structure of creation, and for present purposes it is helpful to hold in mind the poet's progress through the nine circles of hell and, subsequently, the stages of purgatory and paradise. Dante's poem is unique in its completeness and circumstantial detail, but Middle English writers were no less steeped in the Ptolemaic-Christian view. As already noted, aspects of the physical system were known in Old English times, but a full understanding of the universe as the book of nature did not become a shaping force on literature until later.

The level of popular understanding of the world view is probably fairly well represented by accounts in the moral treatises, which also set forth the elementary dogmas of Christianity. On the other hand, a few of the more learned

writers, of whom Gower, Lydgate, and especially Chaucer
are obvious examples, possessed a deeper command of the
subject than could have been derived from such sources.
The presentation of the medieval world view that follows is
drawn to a large extent from the popular treatises, but additional details having relevance to literature are also included. The diagrams and tables provided here will facili-
tate the exposition.

The gross anatomy of the Ptolemaic system viewed

Figure 1.   *Typical Pre-Copernican Diagram of the Universe. [Reproduced from Petrus Apianus, Cos-
mographia, Antwerp, 1574. Courtesy of Stanford University Libraries.]*

Table 1. *Explanation of the Diagram of the Universe, Figure 1*

Reading from the outer circle to the center:

The Empyreal Heaven, the Habitations of God and of all the Elect
(Stable, incorruptible, above the realm of time.)

The Tenth Heaven, the First Mover
(The envelope containing the universe which has a clockwise rotation period of 24 hours; the motion is imparted to the 7 planetary spheres.)

The Ninth Heaven, the Crystalline Sphere

The Eighth Heaven, the Firmament or Sphere of the Fixed Stars

The Sphere of Saturn
(Counter-clockwise rotation period of about 30 years.)

The Sphere of Jupiter
(Counter-clockwise rotation period of about 12 years.)

The Sphere of Mars
(Counter-clockwise rotation period of about 2 years.)

The Sphere of the Sun
(Counter-clockwise rotation period of 1 year; the "King of the planets.")

The Sphere of Venus
(Counter-clockwise rotation period of 224 days.)

The Sphere of Mercury
(Counter-clockwise rotation period of 88 days.)

The Sphere of the Moon
(Counter-clockwise rotation period of 27⅓ days.)

The Belt of Fire

The Belt of Air

Earth
(A stationary globe at the center of the universe, smaller than any of the other planets save the moon; the earth and all that exists on earth, animate and inanimate, are a corruptible compound of the four elements—fire, air, water, and earth.)

from above is represented in a sixteenth-century drawing, Figure 1; and Table 1 identifies the more important parts of the world machine. It may be seen that the immovable center of the system is the earth, of which the water-girt habitable portion is pictured. The surrounding clouds are meant to indicate that the earth's blanket of air extends upward to a belt of fire, the lightest of the four elements. The planetary spheres, which revolve in a celestial gas called aether, envelop the earth with its belts of air and fire in the order indicated in both the diagram and the table. The planets Uranus and Neptune, it may be parenthetically noted, were not discovered until the nineteenth century and Pluto not until 1930. Beyond lies the sphere or firmament of the fixed stars, and the drawing also shows the "crystalline sphere," a corrective concept introduced to help explain the phenomenon known as the precession of the equinoxes. Embracing the whole is the Primum Mobile or First Mover, here labeled the "tenth heaven." The habitations of God, the saints, and the elect souls lie beyond in the empyrean. The zodiacal and planetary signs used by the ancient astronomers are also shown in the drawing.

The apparent motions of the heavenly bodies as seen from the stationary and centrally located earth may best be explained with the aid of another diagram (Figure 2) showing a "side" view of the sun's course. To an observer in the northern hemisphere, the sun seems to cross the southern sky from east to west, reaching its zenith at midsummer and its nadir, or lowest point on the horizon, in winter. In each period of twenty-four hours, not only the moon, but the other planets as well, may be observed to follow closely the path, the ecliptic, marked out by the sun, although they proceed at differing rates of speed. Taken all together, the courses of the seven planets fall within a narrow belt known as the Zodiac not more than 16 degrees in width. This diurnal sweep of the planets about the earth and, of course, the alternation of day and night, are accounted for in the Ptolemaic system by giving to the Primum Mobile a twenty-four hour period of rotation in a clockwise direc-

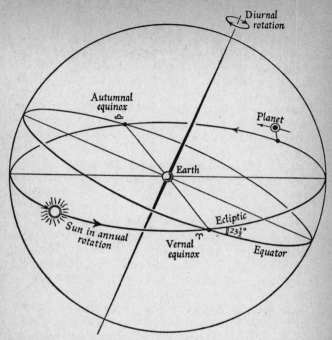

Figure 2. *The Diurnal and Annual Motions of the Sun.*
[*Reproduced from* The Equatorie of the Plan-
etis, *Derek J. Price and R. M. Wilson, eds.
(Cambridge, Eng.: University Press, 1955), 96.
By permission of the publisher.*]

tion, a motion which is imparted to the seven planetary
spheres.

As may be seen in Figure 2, the sun is conceived of
being so affixed to its sphere that its twenty-four hour orbit
is tilted 23½ degrees out of the plane of the earth's equator. The same is true, of course, of the closely grouped orbits of the other planets, although they are not shown in
the diagram. Because of the tilt of the planetary orbits rela-

tive to the earth's equator and the celestial axis, the imaginary belt called the Zodiac describes a thwart-wise or shuttling course around the earth. In visualizing this concept, it is helpful to think of the Zodiac as a narrow band inscribed on the inside surface of the diurnally-revolving Primum Mobile. To the observer, the position of the belt as defined by the transit of the planets constantly changes its elevation in the sky. In any twenty-four hour period, the Zodiac shifts from its lowest position toward the horizon to a point 23½ degrees higher in the sky and back again, the high point and the low point being dependent on the latitude of the observer. In the northern hemisphere, the Zodiac spans the southern sky, and the reverse is true, of course, in the southern hemisphere. For any given latitude, the up and down shift of the Zodiac each twenty-four hours remains a constant throughout the year.

As an aid to charting the heavens, the Zodiac from very ancient times has been divided into 12 arcs of equal magnitude (30 degrees) to each of which is traditionally given the name and sign of a constellation—namely, Aries the Ram, Taurus the Bull, Gemini the Twins, Cancer the Crab, Leo the Lion, Virgo the Virgin, Libra the Scales, Scorpio the Scorpion, Sagittarius the Archer, Capricornus the Goat, Aquarius the Water Carrier, and Pisces the Fishes. The portion or arc of the Zodiac which, as viewed from any point in the northern hemisphere, most nearly approaches the zenith is Cancer; that which is found lowest on the horizon is Capricornus.

The seven planetary spheres may not be regarded as inertly submissive to the twenty-four hour rotation of the Primum Mobile. If this were true, the planets would remain always in the same sign of the Zodiac and would bear a constant relationship to each other as viewed from the earth. Moreover, no seasonal changes would take place, and the moon would not go through its phases. The persistent changes in the relative positions of the planets and all the consequent phenomena are accounted for by giving to each planetary sphere a counter-clockwise rotation at its own rate of speed. The sphere of the sun completes one such revolution in a year, that of the moon in 27⅓ days, and the other planets from somewhat less than two years (Mars) to approximately thirty years (Saturn). Because of their independent motion, the planets to man on earth seem to travel in a counter-clockwise direction through the signs of the Zodiac. When the sun in its annual peregrination reaches that section of the Zodiac called Cancer, it is carried to its highest point in the sky in the northern hemisphere and the season there is summer, and as it continues into Leo and Virgo its height decreases and the days gradually become shorter. Table 2, indicating the progression of the sun through the Zodiac, may be useful at this point.

Table 2.   *The Progression of the Sun*

SUN ENTERS

♈ 1. Aries (Ram) 21 March
♉ 2. Taurus (Bull) 20 April
♊ 3. Gemini (Twins) 21 May
♋ 4. Cancer (Crab) 22 June
♌ 5. Leo (Lion) 23 July
♍ 6. Virgo (Virgin) 23 August
♎ 7. Libra (Balance) 23 September
♏ 8. Scorpio (Scorpion) 24 October
♐ 9. Sagittarius (Archer) 22 November
♑ 10. Capricornus (Goat) 22 December
♒ 11. Aquarius (Water Bearer) 20 January
♓ 12. Pisces (Fishes) 19 February

Thus, by positing a diurnal rotation of the planetary spheres, the Ptolemaic system explains the alternation of day and night and the rising and setting of the other heavenly bodies, and by giving an independent movement to each of the planets it provides an equally clear accounting for seasonal changes and such other phenomena as the phases of the moon and the tides of the ocean. When continued observation disclosed certain irregularities, additional refinements in the movements of the spheres had to be postulated. For example, it was noted that the sun does not proceed through the twelve signs of the Zodiac at a constant speed. That is, its path from the vernal to the autumnal equinox requires a week longer than its subsequent journey from the autumnal back to the vernal position. To account for this aberration, astronomers assumed that the sun's path is slightly eccentric rather than perfectly circular. To explain analogous discrepancies in the behavior of other planets, the theory of epicycles was developed. That is, instead of being fastened firmly to the surface of its sphere, the planet was understood to pursue a circular orbit at one speed or another about a center on the sphere. Figure 3 represents in a general way the epicycles of the planets.

Of the so-called fixed stars, approximately 1022 visible to the naked eye in the nothern hemisphere are listed and plotted in the early star catalogues. Polaris, called the North Star because of its proximity to the projection of the earth's axis on the celestial sphere, was of great importance, especially for navigation. The fixed stars, as indicated in Figure 1, are consigned in the Ptolemaic universe to a sphere of their own, but the phenomenon of the precession of the equinoxes made necessary a modification of the concept of immovable stars. Precession refers to the very slow motion of the earth's axis: instead of pointing always at Polaris, the axis seems to describe a circle on the celestial sphere, completing the cycle in a period computed by the ancients as 36,000 years but now known to be more nearly 26,000 years. To explain this movement, the sphere of the fixed stars was given a counter-clockwise rotation at the rate of 1 degree per 100 years. An apparent variability in the rate of precession led later to the insertion of one and sometimes two crystalline or transparent spheres between the Primum Mobile and the celestial sphere.

By the sixteenth century, the Ptolemaic theory, adjusted and elaborated to account for the more recently observed inequalities, had become extremely complex. The

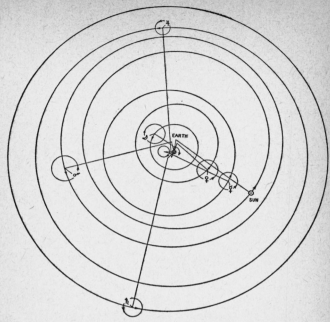

Figure 3.   The Epicycles of the Planets. [*Reproduced from Galileo Galilei*, Dialogue on the Great World Systems, *Giorgio Santillana, ed. (Chicago, Ill.: University of Chicago Press, 1953), p. xvi, Fig. 1. Copyright © 1953 by The University of Chicago Press. By permission of the publisher.*]

time was ripe, it would seem, for the great work, *On the Revolutions of the Celestial Orbs*, 1543, in which Copernicus, returning to the heliocentric system of the ancients and giving to the earth two motions—rotation on its own axis and an orbit about the sun—presented a somewhat simplified mathematical model of the universe.[6] Conservative churchmen were deeply antagonistic toward the new astronomy, as is reflected in the persecution of Kepler, the condemnation by the Holy Office of Copernicus's book, and the forced retraction of Galileo. This consternation arose in part from fear that the new concepts were opposed to Holy Scripture: if the earth moves, how could Joshua have commanded the sun and moon to stand still? More important was the growing recognition that the Copernican theory and the fresh observations it engendered were bringing about the destruction of the natural philosophy and the celestial mechanics of Aristotle to which the old system was wedded. And finally, the complex of divine analogies through which it was held that God made known his purposes to man on earth was seen to be threatened. As the poet John Donne said: "and new Philosophy calls all in doubt."

In the large body of popular didactic writing, *The South English Legendary*, a widely-circulated compilation of saints' lives dating from the late thirteenth century, unexpectedly preserves one of the most nearly complete vernacular accounts of the medieval universe. In the very midst of marvelous hagiographic stories about Sebastian, Valentine, Matthew, Chad, Cuthbert, Brendan, and many others, the author inserts a lengthy discourse on the Archangel Michael. The account of Michael's role in putting the rebellious Lucifer out of heaven and casting him into the pit of hell leads to a description of various features of the universe and a discussion of man's place therein. So much standard lore important to English literature of the period is incorporated in this work that it deserves a closer characterization.

First are described the fall of Lucifer and his minions through pride, their expulsion from heaven, and confinement in hell. The less depraved among the sinful angels still inhabit parts of the earth and, in the form of elves, tend to threaten man if he is unwary. Second, the race of man, created to fill the thrones vacated by the lost tenth order of angels, also was condemned to hell through our first father's sin and would have remained there irrevocably had not Christ bought their souls from the Devil. Third, we are told that hell is a pit in the center of the earth. On its part, the earth is like an apple in shape and of a size much inferior to that of all the other planets save the moon. The order in which the planets encircle the earth is given us, and the heaven of fixed stars is said to enclose the whole system. Some notion of astronomical distances is provided in a number of quaint observations. The distance from the moon to the sun, the king of the planets, is more than three times that separating the earth from the moon. The outer celestial sphere is unimaginably far off: if Adam upon his creation had begun traveling straight up at the rate of forty miles per day, he would not even yet have reached that sphere. The reason human souls on their liberation from the body can ever attain to heaven, which lies beyond the fixed stars, is that spirits are able to move with the speed of thought.

The listing of the planets appears to have inspired the writer's digression on the naming of the weekdays and also on the influences, especially the evil influence of Mars and Saturn, on men. Nevertheless, it is argued that a man of good conscience ("of god inwit") does not necessarily yield to such promptings, for planets do no more than suggest evil or good in a man's will.

Fourth, scattered remarks are offered on the four elements—earth, water, air, and fire—of which all creation below the moon is composed. By showing how the heat of the sun draws water and dust into the upper air, the author accounts for rainfall, snow, hail, thunder, and lightning. The devils are terrified of thunder, he avers, because to them it is reminiscent of the crucifixion and of the subsequent breaking down of hell's gates by Christ. He goes on to say that the sun's heat is so unevenly distributed on the earth that only one-seventh of its surface is habitable. Man's elemental body is also treated as are the consequences with respect to the individual's personality and physical appearance of a superfluity of one element or the other. Whoever is composed of too much air, for example, is fat, a great fool and lecher, and yet a happy man.

Finally, we learn that, soon after conception, the human fetus is comprised of three connected balls which become respectively the liver, heart, and brain. The liver is the seat of the natural soul, which furnishes nourishment to the whole body; the vital soul in the heart is the principle underlying the five senses; and the third soul in the brain, usually called the animal soul, or *virtus animalis,* is described here as the master of the other two. Into it, at the end of the fourth month of fetal life, the Lord infuses the nature of heaven—that is, the wit and will of the angels. This soul may not die, but upon the extinction of the body and the other two souls it proceeds either to joy or woe forever. It is that which distinguishes man from all other denizens of the earth and allies him to the angels.[7] A somewhat more technical treatment of the "souls" of man appears in the compendium of Bartholomeus Anglicus.[8]

Another work incorporating popular instruction about the universe and man is the mid-thirteenth-century *Image du Monde,* translated by Caxton in 1481 as *The Mirrour of the World.* This encyclopedic book opens with an encomium on Christian clerks and the seven liberal arts—grammar, logic, rhetoric, arithmetic, geometry, music, and astronomy—by means of which we understand something of God's creation. Grammar is the gate to the other arts, the foundation and beginning of "clergy" or learning, for it was by the "Word" that God created the heavens and earth. Arithmetic is discussed from the Ptolemaic viewpoint as the mediator between the physical world and theology. Astronomy, however, is the true end of clergy, for, embracing all the other arts, it studies the whole of nature. Indeed, God himself is the great Astronomer; by a knowledge of astronomy man is converted to a belief in God. The treatise thereafter provides a brief and simplified description of the universe, likening it to a pellet in the very center of which stands the earth, likewise spherical in shape. *The Mirrour* emphasizes the minuteness of the earth in comparison with the universe. Other writers stress even more its insignificance, noting that it occupies the lowest place and that it is in the realm of corruptible matter, the dregs of creation. Although one-quarter of the earth, rather than only one-seventh, as is sometimes conjectured, is inhabited, one should not be so naïve as to assume that a man or beast would fall off if placed on the opposite side of the globe.

Surrounding the earth concentrically are the several spheres, the first seven bearing the planets and the eighth carrying the fixed stars. The dual motion of the planets in relation to the earth is rather skillfully described in *The Mirrour*. The heavens move about the earth in a day and a night pulling along the sun like a nail affixed in a wheel. Yet, because the position of the sun varies from day to day, it must be likened not to a nail but rather to a fly which crawls slowly around the wheel in a direction contrary to that of rotation. Also included is a commentary on the four elements. A ring of fire encloses the envelope of air about the earth just as the white of an egg encloses the yolk. Further, one finds here much traditional lore about such matters as the location of the earthly paradise, the regions of the earth, and the inhabitants, mythological and otherwise.[9]

Another moral work almost encyclopedic in scope is Guillaume de Deguileville's treatise of the first half of the fourteenth century, translated by John Lydgate in 1426 under the title *The Pilgrimage of the Life of Man*. The human soul is said here to move contrary to the impulses of the body and thus provides an analogue to the counter motion of each of the planets with respect to the revolution of the Primum Mobile. The man who contemplates this analogy will be strengthened in virtuous perseverance. One of the experiences of the narrator in this dream-vision allegory is of particular interest. The beautiful lady Grace Dieu temporarily releases his soul from the confines of his body and allows it to soar aloft and thus experience the joy of disencumberment from the crass flesh. This heavenly journey is in some ways reminiscent of the ascent to the throne of God undertaken by Prudence in the *Anti-Claudianus* of Alanus de Lille (died c. 1203), although Alanus is more aware of astronomical phenomena. A treatment of fortune and of astrological influences is also included in *The Pilgrimage*. God gave the celestial bodies only as signs to the end that man may recognize that he is the microcosm. The planets are credited with exerting forces on the denizens of earth, but Ptolemy is quoted to the effect that a wise man has dominion over his fate above that of the heavens.[10]

Aspects or fragments of the world view are imbedded in many other didactic works. *The Pricke of Conscience*, in the course of remarks about "Dam Fortone" and her ever-turning wheel, urges that worldly success is to be dreaded; it is even a sign of damnation. Sorrow and tribulation, on the other hand, are to be welcomed because they cleanse man from sin. In this same vein, the author notes that this world is fast approaching its end, as clerks know by certain tokens. He further gives emphasis to the macrocosm-microcosm idea when remarking that man, the lesser world, has the shape and likeness of the greater world.[11] In his instructional poem on the Trinity, William of Shoreham muses on the stability of the earth as opposed to the restless motion of the planets and concludes that only an all-powerful God could sustain such a system. The hand of God, he says, may be seen in every facet of his creation.[12]

However fully and interestingly the authors of the popular compendia reviewed above represent the world view in its broad features, there remain a few organically related topics with which they do not deal in sufficient detail for the enlightenment of modern readers. Since some of these topics, as acknowledged above, figure prominently in the works of English poets of superior learning, a comment about each seems to be in order. The most important topics are (1) the Providence of God versus man's free will; (2) Providence, destiny, and fortune, both general and personal; and (3) the doctrine of the humors, medieval medicine, and predictive astrology. Despite its close kinship to the last of these three subjects, alchemy, or the supposed science of transmuting base metals into gold, will not be treated here. Chaucer's *Canon's Yeoman's Tale* represents the most important use of alchemical lore in Middle English literature.

1. The Providence of God Versus Man's Free Will

Chaucer and other writers were fond of reminding their audiences that a conflict arises between the concepts of God as an omniscient and just being and of free will as a function of man's soul. It appears unjust for God to permit individuals to fall into mortal sin when he could prevent their going to hell. Indeed, the fact that God in his omniscience knows that many are reprobated seems to require us to say that he predestines men before their birth to salvation or reprobation. In effect, then, the freedom of man's will is illusory. Perhaps the most effective and distinguished passage in English literature involving this motif is Troilus's soliloquy in the temple in the latter part of Chaucer's *Troilus and Criseyde*. For artistic reasons, Chaucer allows Troilus to lash out bitterly against the destiny that foresaw his loss of Criseyde, and then withheld from him any inkling of the Christian resolution of the dilemma.[13] It will be remembered from the short discussion of Boethius in an earlier chapter that *The Consolation* sets forth the answer exonerating God from malevolence and offering some solace to believers. Because he dwells outside the realm of time, God's knowledge—which only to us is *fore*knowledge—is completely and necessarily true, but it does not follow that God's knowledge is from his standpoint a prejudgment. It is rather that God knows how every man will use his free will because in the eternal mind every man's life has already been lived. The question may still be asked why the universe is so ordered that some men are condemned to hell, but the final answer lies beyond the understanding of man.

2. Providence, Destiny, and Fortune

God's Providence is a very broad concept embracing the divine plan as expressed in the whole of creation including the heavenly kingdom for all eternity. Although often used rather loosely as synonyms for each other and also for Providence, the terms "destiny" and "fortune" also had more limited and distinctive senses. The term "fate," on the other hand, appears never to have been consistently used except in a generalized way. Destiny was considered to be that part of Providence which underlies all movable creation from the planets down to the lowliest manifestations of nature on earth. Fortune, a further subdivision, was conceived as administering the decrees of destiny applying particularly to human beings. Two kinds of fortune were conventionally distinguished: first, "general fortune," also called "simple necessity" by Boethius, which sets the conditions of life imposed on man as a species—his progress from birth to old age, his method of procreation including the period of gestation, his average life span, and the like; and second, "personal fortune," or Boethius's "conditional necessity," which concerns the life experiences of a given individual.[14]

The differences between general and personal fortune are at issue in a passage in the Epistle of James, 1:13-14, and in a remark citing these Biblical verses given by Chaucer to the Clerk of Oxford at the conclusion of his tale about the Patient Griselda. The gist of the passage is that no man may claim that he is tempted to sin by God, for when he falls into sin, "he is drawn away of his own lust, and enticed." Sin always begins as a motion of man's will and therefore is part of personal fortune. On the other hand, man is tested or "proved," to use Chaucer's word, as a result of general fortune—namely, his membership in the species man which means that he is endowed with an elemental body and also free will.[15] The astrological implications of personal fortune are touched on in the following paragraphs.

3. The Humors, Medieval Medicine, and Predictive Astrology

The early Christians tended to condemn astrology, along with pagan soothsayers, augurers, magicians, and other oracles, because, by subjecting men to celestial influences, it seemed to leave no scope for the operation of the free will. Astrology, in other words, led too easily to absolute determinism. Among non-Christians, astrology was very popular, although there were some like Cicero who attacked its pretentions on the grounds of common sense. The problem presented by the twins who, despite their being born under the same disposition of the heavens, experience quite different fortunes was often urged as a refutation of predictive astrology. After the fall of Rome, astrological science waned, although some rudimentary recognition of the significance of the heavens persisted, perhaps because of allusions to the stars as signs in the Bible, as in Genesis 1:14. The *Saxon Chronicle*, written in England during the period 891 to 1154, refers to comets, bloody rains, and crosses in the sky as portents, but the fully developed theories of Ptolemy seem not to have been known. Bede alludes to certain phases of the subject only, and another Englishman at the close of the Old English period, Ælfric (c. 955-1020), cites the old argument of the twins in an attack on astrological superstition.

The Arabians fell heir to the science of Ptolemy during the Dark Ages in western Europe just as they did to the works of the philosophers. In this milieu, astrology came to be associated with demonology and necromancy. From Arabic Spain, astrology returned to western Christendom in the twelfth and thirteenth centuries. By this time, the science had absorbed not only demonology but also some elements of the cosmology of Aristotle—in particular, his doctrine of the fifth essence, the refined incorruptible material of which the planets were considered to be made. When purified of demonology to some extent, this refurbished astrology came to be somewhat more acceptable to Christians than it had been in the days of the early Fathers. Moreover, a rationale was devised to relieve it of some of the determinism that was so repugnant to Christians. From this time, astrology was widely accepted in Europe even though most moralists remained aware of the lingering danger of determinism.

Ptolemy's formulation of the science was crucial. Taking over the Greek theory of the four elements, he placed each of the planets in control of one or another of the elements. As Table 3 indicates, the planet Mars, when in certain signs of the Zodiac (Aries, Leo, or Sagittarius) has a strong effect on fire; Saturn, when in Taurus, Virgo, or Capricornus, influences earth; and so on.[16]

The medical applications of this concept are of special interest. Because man has an elemental body, he is, of course, subject to planetary influences. The old doctrine of the four humors or bodily fluids which have their seats in various organs, as indicated in Table 3, fits easily into the whole scheme because each humor is associated with a particular element and is assigned properties supposed to characterize that element. Choler or yellow bile, rising in the gall bladder, is equated with fire and is thus considered to give off heat and dryness to the whole body. The other humors are similarly analyzed. When his humors are mixed in exactly the right proportions, a man is not only physically healthy but his personality (temperament, or mixture) too is in balance. An imbalance of humors, however, results in bodily and sometimes also in mental disorder.

The physician's task was not only to treat his patient empirically but also to be aware of the planetary influences on his condition. Properly to do this, he needed to know the disposition of the heavens at the time of the patient's birth and the present position of the relevant heavenly bodies. His medicine had to be administered at the astro-

Table 3. *The Medieval Theory of the Humors**

Element	Qualities	Humor	Complexion	Signs of Zodiac corresponding to element	Planet possessing corresponding qualities
Fire	Hot and Dry	Choler (yellow bile)	Choleric (irascible, passionate, bilious)	Aries Leo Sagittarius	Mars (the lesser evil)
Earth	Cold and Dry	Melancholy (black bile)	Melancholic (sullen, dejected, bad tempered)	Taurus Virgo Capricornus	Saturn (the greater evil)
Air	Hot and Moist	Blood	Sanguine (ardent, cheerful, venereal, liberal)	Gemini Libra Aquarius	Jupiter (the greater fortune)
Water	Cold and Moist	Phlegm	Phlegmatic (cold, dull, apathetic, cool, calm)	Cancer Scorpio Pisces	Venus (the lesser fortune)

* By courtesy of the late Francis R. Johnson.

logically correct hour to exert its full effect and help restore the patient's balance of humors. Practicing physicians must have differed a good deal in their reliance on the planets and their use of astrological talismans, but certainly Chaucer's Doctor of Physic was a believer in this form of treatment.[17]

Along with astrological medicine and such other technical fields as alchemy, predictive astrology came to be widely known and practiced. Two types of prognostication were distinguished: first, general prognostication, which was the science of predicting momentous events, such as war, pestilence, earthquakes, unfavorable weather, and the like, which would affect a large aggregate of men; and second, individual prognostication, which was the forecasting of the future vicissitudes of an individual. For the purposes of prediction, certain planets were regarded as good or fortunate (Jupiter and Venus), others as bad (Saturn and Mars), and one as changeable (Mercury, hence our term "mercurial"). Further elaborations were the assigning of masculine and feminine gender to both the planets and constellations, and the complex distinctions made among "aspects" or the relationships of the heavenly bodies to one another. In casting a horoscope, the astrologer determined the positions of the planets at the moment of his client's birth, a task of some delicacy. Each constellation was considered to rule over a particular phase of life, such as marriage, wealth, and sickness. If an evil planet (Saturn or Mars) stood in the mansion of wealth, the client's lot would be poverty. The planets were regarded as exerting a paramount influence on personal fortune and the fixed stars were sometimes viewed as significant as far as general prognostication was concerned.[18]

. . . . . .

The vast complex of whirling spheres just described was only the objectification of the medieval world view. Considered in all its aspects, this concept offered a kind of unified field theory expressing the organic relationship of man on earth to religious truths, or the place of man in God's Providence. It accommodated all that man is permitted to learn by his own efforts and boldly linked that knowledge to what he knows through divine revelation. The music produced by the rotating spheres was only the prelude to the harmonies of heaven lying in illimitable space beyond the Primum Mobile. Mirroring the symmetry of the great world, the macrocosm, and answering to some of the same laws was man, the little world or microcosm. A compound of observable fact, of philosophy, of theology, and of poetry, this all-enveloping construct was the prime source of religious awe, of artistic inspiration, and, moreover, of the idiom or imagery of the medieval imagination. Today, we are likely to think of life in the Middle Ages too exclusively in terms of its primitive technology, of its presumed intellectual impoverishment, or of brutally hard social and economic conditions. When it comes to products of the medieval mind, however, we must be constantly aware that within the purview of the least of men in this age of belief glimmered the hope of heaven—a hope that was endorsed and authenticated not only by the liturgy and teachings of the Church but also by the whole of visible creation.

Some knowledge of English medieval society and cultural history is obviously essential to an understanding of numberless more or less specialized terms and allusions in Old and Middle English literature. But beyond supplying the reader with a gloss on such explicit matters, the present book, it is hoped, will convey an appreciation of medieval religiosity, of the integrated world view of the times, as it existed in England. For deeply imbued with this religious spirit were attitudes on subjects that are basic in the literature of all ages—for example, the characteristic attitudes toward adversity, toward death, toward love, and toward nature.

FURTHER READINGS

Curry, Walter Clyde, *Chaucer and the Mediæval Sciences*, 2nd ed., New York: Barnes & Noble, 1960.

Johnson, Francis R., *Astronomical Thought in Renaissance England*, Baltimore, Md.: The Johns Hopkins Press, 1937.

Kuhn, Thomas S., *The Copernican Revolution: Planetary Astronomy in the Development of Western Thought*, Cambridge, Mass.: Harvard University Press, 1957.

Mazzeo, Joseph Anthony, *Medieval Cultural Tradition in Dante's Comedy*, Ithaca, N. Y.: Cornell University Press, 1960.

Thorndike, Lynn, *A History of Magic and Experimental Science During the First Thirteen Centuries of Our Era*, 2 vols., New York: The Macmillan Company, 1929.

Appendix:
Critical Approaches

Concentration on backgrounds —on historical and philological considerations of the sort treated in this book—may all too easily result, and in fact has often resulted, in a fatal neglect of the literature which a knowledge of backgrounds is supposed to illuminate. Clearly, to regard *Beowulf* primarily as a storehouse of Germanic cognates or as an exemplification of a particular theory of epic composition is to miss the literary experience which the poem offers the reader. The act of criticism, of formulating a responsible and informed judgment or evaluation, is no less binding when the work in question happens to have been written in the eighth rather than in the twentieth century and in Old English rather than in the modern idiom. As an epilogue to this book, then, a commentary on various critical approaches to English medieval literature is in order.

When it comes to expressing his reactions to the writings of the Middle Ages, the modern reader is likely to regret the absence of direct notices of those works by medieval critics. It is true that one may glean from later poets a few encomia on their contemporaries or near-contemporaries, such as Hoccleve's praise of Chaucer. Moreover, the moralists were fond of passing severe judgment on the turpitude of romance writers and minstrels. Such comments, however, are too few and trifling to support any true evaluations. Criticism, in the proper sense of the term, did not evolve in England until the sixteenth century, the day of Wilson and Ascham, when vernacular literature had begun to achieve respectability in the eyes of the educated. Since then, every period and every movement has had its chroniclers, prophets, theorists, and detractors, some of whom have simultaneously gained distinction as critics and writers. It is not only that Thomas Wilson's *Arte of Rhetorique*, John Dryden's *Essay of Dramatick Poesie*, Samuel Johnson's *Lives of the Poets*, Samuel Taylor Coleridge's *Biographia Literaria*, and T. S. Eliot's "The Function of Criticism" are landmarks of intellectual and cultural history and are also literary works in their own right. Beyond this, they supply us with insights into the literature of their own times in a way that has become almost indispensable to us. Even if we do not accept Johnson's evaluation of *Lycidas* or *Gulliver's Travels*, we profit greatly from his formulation of the standards of his day when we make the effort to shape our own understanding of these works.

The lack of comparable discussions of English literature in the Middle Ages has naturally prompted scholars to study tangential sources of enlightenment about the "intentions" of and contemporaneous attitudes toward medieval writers. In other words, critics of the early monuments of English literature inevitably rely to an extraordinary degree on background information, on their understanding of the life and thought of the age. They tend to hold that a critical grasp of pre-sixteenth-century works must be based upon or at least must take seriously into account such specialized subjects as (1) medieval rhetorical theory, (2) source studies, (3) folklore, myth, and ritual, or (4) Scriptural allegory. Each of these approaches will be briefly characterized.

1. Rhetorical Theory

The rhetorical approach is treated first because, of all the writings surviving from the Middle Ages, the rhetorics and grammars come closest in matter and purpose to the later criticism. That is, they deal to some extent with literary creation and even literary theory even though they do not proceed to a direct critique of contemporaneous authors.

The relevance of rhetorical principles to the analysis and understanding of the older literature of England has been vigorously asserted since the 1920's, when a well-known edition of medieval "arts of poetry" [1] was followed closely by J. M. Manly's famous lecture "Chaucer and the Rhetoricians," [2] and then by many other investigations of the possible influence of rhetorical concepts on English writers. *Beowulf* and other Old English poems, it has been argued, reveal the shaping effects of a knowledge of such principles of ancient rhetoric as amplification.[3] Chaucer's entire career has been depicted in terms of an early dependence on the precepts of rhetoricians and then a later tendency to "throw away the rule book," as in his *General Prologue*, in which his portraits of the pilgrims depart from the patterns recommended by the theorists.[4] Again, *Piers Plowman* is said to bespeak a familiarity with a special development of rhetoric, the preaching manuals, and also with actual sermons of the period.[5]

Supporting the acceptance of this kind of influence is the view that all educated men would have studied rhetoric as the second of the seven liberal arts forming the school curriculum throughout most of the Middle Ages. Rhetoric, in fact, is a member of the Trivium, along with grammar and logic. Further, rhetoric, at least that of later times, is often regarded as embracing treatises on poetic composition, such as those of Geoffroi de Vinsauf and Matthieu de Vendôme, both thirteenth-century Englishmen. Very recently, the doctrine of rhetorical study has been challenged on the grounds that rhetoric, or at any rate the species represented by the "arts of poetry," was probably not part of the school curriculum and that such works cannot have been widely known in England before the fifteenth century. What knowledge poets had of figures, tropes, and colors of rhetoric, it is argued, could easily have been acquired from the grammar texts of Donatus and others, whereas Chaucer's acquaintance with Geoffroi de Vinsauf ("O Gaufred, deere maister soverayn" [6]) could have reached him through a well-known Latin chronicle which includes a brief excerpt from Geoffroi's art of poetry.[7]

Whether English poets knew the formal treatises on poetic composition at first hand and followed their precepts in composing their own works is a question that need not be settled here. The fact remains that the Latin grammatical and rhetorical works by medieval Englishmen offer some testimony about literary knowledge and attitudes of the times that is occasionally useful in the evaluation of vernacular writings. That is, we learn from such sources what classical authors were favored and to some extent how they were viewed. Within such limits, an understanding of the rhetorical tradition certainly contributes to our interpretation of literature.[8]

2. Source Studies

One species of historical criticism, the investigation of literary sources, has in recent years been occasionally under fire.[9] The aim here is to offer a few remarks on this approach and, by the citing of examples, to suggest that a detailed knowledge of what a given author does with his immediate sources has sometimes contributed to our grasp of his work.

Examples of the most fruitful source studies come from the Middle English rather than the earlier period chiefly because the origins of that body of literature are more certainly identifiable. One may begin with the excellent fourteenth-century romance known as *Ywain and*

Gawain, which without doubt was taken directly from
Yvain, ou le Chevalier au Lion, considered by some to be
Chrétien de Troyes' masterpiece. A reader familiar with
the tenor of the Old French romance will note at once
that, however close in plot details, in total effect the English *Ywain* differs markedly from its original. This differ-
ence results at least in part from the English poet's deletion
of Chrétien's playful or fanciful commentary on the action,
his epic similes, and his elaborate character analysis. Moreover, the plot action is somewhat simplified in the deriva-
tive work. These observations are likely to tempt one to
write off *Ywain and Gawain* as the work of a bourgeois
poet incapable of coping with the psychological refinements
or the stylistic nuances of his courtly original. But a closer
comparison of the two and also some knowledge about the
genre of Middle English romance will serve as a corrective.
That is, it will become clear that the suppression of
Chrétien's musing on his characters, the insertion of
homely English proverbs, and, in general, the shunning of
the high style of the French were cleanly and systematically
carried out by the Englishman. The result is a virile,
straightforward tale which conforms to the English prefer-
ence in romances. Knightly idealism is not lost because of
the English poet's omission of the lengthy internal mono-
logues to be found in the French but, especially in the duel
between the hero and Gawain, is allowed to express itself in
overt action. The virtues of *Ywain and Gawain* lie in a
somewhat different sphere from those of Chrétien's *Yvain,*
then, but they are none the less virtues. One critic, at least,
regards the English poem as definitely superior as literature
to its original.[10]

Another fourteenth-century work our full appreciation
of which may be said to be advanced as the result of source
studies is Chaucer's *Troilus and Criseyde.* It is true that
some notion of the greatness of this work is likely to be
apparent at once to the most uninstructed reader. But with
almost equal certainty his appreciation of the depth of
Chaucer's characterizations will be enhanced by compari-

son with the relatively crude, black and white principals in Boccaccio's *Filostrato*. Again, without some knowledge of the Italian original, one is likely to miss the real force of Chaucer's importation of Boethian philosophizing and therefore much of the moral and spiritual elevation of the poem. The passages in which such ideas figure most effectively are Troilus's soliloquy over the prospective loss of Criseyde and the palinode uttered by his spirit at the close of the poem.[11]

Other examples of the benefits of source studies could readily be cited. Thus, the entire question of whether Sir Thomas Malory's *Le Morte Darthur* was written as a single, thematically-unified work, as R. M. Lumiansky and others have argued,[12] or as a collection of eight rather loosely-connected romances, as the editor Eugène Vinaver believes,[13] hangs to some extent on careful investigations of Malory's several sources and the use he made of his material. A considerable advance has also taken place in recent years in our understanding of the Holy Grail story, the legend which from its emergence in the twelfth century reshaped the entire Arthurian cycle in terms of a great spiritual quest and raised it to an importance virtually unmatched in world literature. It is interesting to note that the concept of the purely Christian origins of the Grail in the Arthurian romances has been effectively questioned by many scholars, especially R. S. Loomis. That is, the Grail episode in Chrétien's unfinished *Perceval* is explained in terms of pagan Celtic *données*. Only later did Chrétien's continuators identify the pagan talisman of *Perceval* with the cup of the Last Supper and the chalice of the Mass.[14]

3. Folklore, Myth, and Ritual

By and large, the studies cited above concern available literary sources. But by no means lacking are arguments based ultimately on hypothetical sources. In their quest for origins, nineteenth-century students sometimes reconstructed in elaborate particularity both the missing links needed for establishing relationships among existing texts and also the aboriginal form, the *Ursage*, of a literary work. Some philologists of the last century not only endorsed the older and now largely rejected theory that *Beowulf* was made up of several separately-composed lays but they also felt justified in specifying the exact subject matter of each lay and describing the contribution of each of several poets who were assumed to have fit them together to form a single epic.[15]

Medievalists of more recent times are not so certain about the validity of such reconstructions even though they are quite as interested in accounting for the subject matter of a work of unknown literary antecedents. A strong tendency is to associate the plot or individual episodes with folk tradition, whether in the form of a folktale, myth, or ritual. Folktales make up an almost limitless body of thrice-told stories which have developed among peoples of all eras, races, and cultures. To speak very generally, folktales seem to fulfill several different functions. Many seek to explain such things as the creation of the world, the origin of life and of man, animal and plant characteristics, meteorological phenomena, and geographical features; some relate humorous anecdotes about wise and stupid beings; and some are meant to edify or move to wonder through fables illustrating common-sense precepts, tales about great heroes of the past, and fantasies concerned with magic and the supernatural. Folktales are generally thought of as the product of primitive cultures, kept alive by oral transmission only, but paradoxically they are known to us today chiefly through literary forms, if we make exception for tales taken down by anthropologists from the lips of native informants.

Some measure of control over this vast corpus of material is provided by a number of comprehensive works,[16] in which tales are catalogued according to numerous general types and also by motifs. Some of the types are Animal Tales, Jokes, Superhuman Tasks, and Magic Objects. The frequently recurring motifs making up the tales include incidents pertaining to the dead, marvels, ogres, reversals of fortune, and the like. The serious study of folklore, which began in the last century with the work of the Grimm brothers, necessitates a careful definition of such terms as "myth." That is, "myth" applies to any ostensibly historical happening involving a religious idea or perhaps a natural phenomenon that is viewed with a kind of religious veneration. The theft of fire, preserved in the story of Prometheus, is a typical myth.[17] One sign of the times is that students of a Freudian or Jungian persuasion have sought to account for existing folktales and especially myths in psychological terms. That is, some folktales are looked upon as dreams common to all human beings bespeaking suppressed desires. The true significance of these symbolic dreams is recoverable only through recourse to a kind of depth psychology. Still another development closely related to myth and altogether relevant to literary criticism is the importance given to "ritual," by which is meant a traditional ceremony or enactment by a community of preliterate people. Rituals are often petitionary in nature, as is true of the rain-making dances of American Indians.

Folklore in its many varieties has been mined in the effort to understand the literature of all ages, but especially that of medieval times, and of such investigations the extensive body of *Beowulf* criticism furnishes excellent examples. The hero Beowulf was once confidently identified as the personification of agriculture and civilization on supposed etymological grounds and his exploits were accordingly considered to be mythic struggles against the elements or representative of seasonal changes. The folklorist Grimm thought that the name Beowulf meant "bee-wolf," or "woodpecker," regarded as a sacred bird by primitive Germanic peoples. Again, much has been written about connections between the *Beowulf* story and the folktale of the Bear's Son, an ancient hero who has a hug like that of a bear and who fights two supernatural beings, one in a house and the other underground. Beowulf's mighty grip and two of his adversaries offer interesting parallels to this tale, and some of the same elements occur in the Old Norse saga *Grettir the Strong*. Another phase of Beowulf's career which is explained by reference to folklore is the unpromising character of his youthful years. For a hero to be known in his early days as unprepossessing or indolent is a widespread notion sometimes referred to as the motif of the Male Cinderella or the Ugly Duckling.[18]

Psychological criticism is sufficiently exemplified by Otto Rank's story of the Griselda legend, in the form which Chaucer adapted from Petrarch in his *Clerk's Tale*. The main plot is held to be basically the Cupid-Psyche story in which a mortal woman marries a god or, as in the Beauty and the Beast variant, a totem animal. The wife can preserve her happiness only by observing a tabu; Psyche was never to inquire into her husband's identity whereas Griselda was bound to be absolutely patient and obedient. Added to this plot in the Griselda story, however, is the denouement in which the husband prepares, or pretends to prepare, to marry his own daughter, an incest motif, according to this point of view.[19]

The resort to ritual observances in literary interpretation is often unsatisfactory owing to the large element of conjecture that is inevitably involved. This difficulty is exemplified in Jessie L. Weston's famous theory which derives the essence of the Grail story from a fertility rite. Specifically, Miss Weston argues that in Chrétien's *Perceval* the events taking place before the hero in the Grail castle—the procession with the Grail and the bleeding lance and the subsequent developments as well—preserve traces of their origin in a folk ceremony depicting the natural processes of decay and new growth, of death and regeneration. Such a rite is assumed to have been maintained well into the Middle Ages in western Europe, although the nearest definite analogue to be found is an Adonis ritual celebrated by the Greeks, based on the myth that Adonis was shared as a lover by Persephone in the Lower World and Aphrodite in the Upper. Mourning accompanied Adonis's departure for Hades in the autumn, the season of decay and death, whereas his return to heaven in the spring signalized joyful new life. The rite underlying the Grail story, it is suggested, must have included the initiation of the hero, Perceval in the Grail story, into the mysteries of life and death. The maiming of the Fisher King—that is, his emasculation—symbolizes death, as does the devastation of the Waste Land. The ultimate healing of the king and the restoration of the land of Logres, of course, represents regeneration. The lance and the Grail brought ceremoniously before the hero are male and female sex symbols.[20] Despite some interesting parallels between this hypothetical ritual and the story of the Holy Grail, most scholars today find Miss Weston's connections too tenuous to compel belief.

Among present-day critics, John Speirs seems to accept the Weston point of view when he asserts that a folk-ritual of some sort underlies Middle English romances such as *Gawain and the Green Knight* and *Gawain and the Carl of Carlisle*. For him, the force of the more striking episodes in these stories, such as the beheading of the "vegetation god" in *Gawain and the Green Knight* and the account of the Carl's charnel house in *Gawain and the Carl of Carlisle*, proceed in some way from the primitivistic energy of an initiation ritual having to do with "the facts of generation." The same critic believes that the assumption of a ritualistic or "anthropological" background provides the best explanation for other "traditional" works, such as certain cycles of mystery plays, and that the alliterative measure of Old and Middle English times is also related to ritual observances.[21] Again, however, the basic problem of establishing the actual existence of such rituals in medieval England is not faced.

4. Allegory

In ancient times, the term "allegory" meant a trope or figure of diction in which one thing is stated in terms of another. As treated by classical rhetoricians, it is closely akin to "metaphor," which is defined as the transferring of a word meaning one thing to something else.[22] Very soon, allegory assumed a more general significance and, thus, could be classified as a figure of thought. It is so used in St. Paul's *Epistle to the Galatians* (4:24-28). In musing about Ishmael and Isaac, the sons respectively of the bond-maid Agar and the free woman Sara, St. Paul says that "these things are an allegory"; they are the two testaments or dispensations, Agar and her children representing Jerusalem, or the old bondage, and the descendants of Sara representing the children of freedom. Here, allegory designates the "spiritual" interpretation as opposed to the literal statement. The similarity of allegory in this meaning to "parable" is at once apparent, although the latter term is commonly employed only in reference to the *exempla* uttered by Christ. Still later, of course, the concept of allegory broadened until it could apply not only to the interpretation of a Biblical passage but to the figurative significance imputed to any secular fiction as well. We are likely to think of allegory today as "extended metaphor," which sometimes makes use of personifications, typical characters, or symbols. Figurative or allegorical expression in the modern sense may be said to lie close to the heart of literature; thus, a primary task of the critic is to assess its effectiveness or appropriateness in a given work.

As has already been shown, medieval literature in general, not merely the work of the mystics, reveals considerable knowledge of the Bible. Beginning in Old English times, vernacular writers paraphrase, quote, and in other ways demonstrate their familiarity with Scripture and occasionally with patristic commentary. One further suspects that a grasp of the general method of Biblical interpretation was fairly general among literate people, at least in the later Middle Ages. All Biblical study was conditioned by two beliefs. First, because it is God's direct revelation to man, the Bible is inerrantly true. Along with all nature, the visible world, it functions as man's guide to charity and salvation when correctly read. Second, Biblical language differs fundamentally from the language of man. That is, the word of God was written out of a perfect knowledge of past, present, and future and of all things mundane and spiritual. The very words of God, then, have meanings extending far beyond any which man can use since man can refer only to events and things in the physical world. It should be noted, however, that the early Biblical commentators were generally considered to have written under special grace, as were the men who penned the books of the Bible, and thus their writings came to acquire a sacrosanct character akin to that of Holy Writ.

These principles coalesce in the view that it was expressly for man's edification that God not only created the universe but ordered the events of Biblical history. One able to read must see that Old Testament events foreshadow those of the New Testament and that both show forth man's ultimate destiny. To return to St. Paul's epistle: God created Agar and Sara as bondmaid and free woman *for the purpose* of revealing to mankind the relationship between the old and the new law.

On the model of such prefigurations written into the Bible, the commentators over the centuries built up a very large body of Scriptural explication, evidently secure in the belief that they were voicing God's intentions. Also, as already suggested, they made distinctions in the kinds of spiritual meanings they set forth. Some writers recognized as many as seven levels of meaning in the word of God, but the famous four levels of exegesis came at length to prevail. These are, first, the literal sense, the message conveyed by the immediate referents of the words; second, the allegorical or historical, illustrated by Old Testament premonitions of New Testament events; third, the tropological or moral, chiefly counsels of perfection; and fourth, the anagogical, statements pertaining to heaven. Thus, in the comments on the name Jerusalem, one may see that, in addition to its direct reference to the religious capital of Palestine, the literal level, it represents allegorically the Church of Christ, as in the Book of Matthew (21:1); tropologically, the faithful soul with its vision of peace, a sense said to be implied in the Gospel of Luke (19), and supported by the etymology of the name; and anagogically, the heavenly city, the

"New Jerusalem" (Gal. 4:26). Other interpretations that figure in medieval literature and art include the identification of Adam as the prefiguration of Christ, the "new Adam," a view encouraged by St. Paul (I Cor. 15:45), of the manna sent down to the children of Israel by Jehovah as the Body of Christ in the Eucharist, of the four-branched river flowing out of Paradise as the four cardinal virtues, and of the householder and his vineyard in the parable of Matthew (20:1-16) as God and his universal Church.

The application to secular literature of the method of analysis that gave rise to such commentaries has produced interesting results. The "polysemous" meanings and the symbolism of Dante's *Divine Comedy* have been expounded almost as if the poem were Holy Writ.[23] Recent Dante scholars tend to emphasize aesthetic rather than purely theological inspiration although they have much to say about whether the poet was consciously using throughout the twofold allegory of secular writers or the fourfold system of the theologians.[24] But Dante is unique in his learning and in voicing his concern with the uses of allegory. Among all the poets of medieval England, only the author of *Piers Plowman* reveals even roughly a similar concern about moral theology and the ways in which God's purposes are subverted in the world of men.

In studies of English literature, the full utilization of exegetical methods is illustrated in the work of several critics. D. W. Robertson, Jr., entertains the conviction that in all poetry by medieval Christians the *sententia* or nucleus embodies a truth that is "always an aspect of charity," however misleading the *cortex* or surface meaning may seem. Such an orientation leads to the expectation that the poet will resort to the four-level presentation in imitation of Scripture. Robertson treats *Pearl*, the great fourteenth-century dream allegory, as a poetic vision intended to persuade the dreamer, who is a typical adult Christian, as well as the audience of the need for regaining the life of innocence or perfect submission to God's will. He then suggests that the Pearl, although a gem on the literal level, conveys this message allegorically through representing all innocents. On the tropological level, the maiden Pearl indicates how one attains innocence, and anagogically she illustrates the life of innocence in heaven.[25] A similar and more circumstantial analysis of *Sir Gawain and the Green Knight* begins with the thesis that the central intent is to provide an edifying fable of the purging of the Round Table of inordinate pride. The corrector is the Green Knight, who is identified allegorically as the voice of God. The axe he carries would have suggested to the original audience John the Baptist's *exemplum* of the axe laid to the root of the "tree which bringeth not forth good fruit" (Matt. 3:10) and also the commentators' discourses on this verse.[26]

Among the several Canterbury tales that have been discussed from this point of view is *The Nun's Priest's Tale*, which has been interpreted as an allegory of the fall of Adam.[27] The Pardoner, as revealed in his prologue and tale, is analyzed as a "spiritual eunuch";[28] and the characterization of old January in *The Merchant's Tale* is likewise thought to reflect a knowledge of Scriptural lore.[29] Moreover, the framing story, the pilgrimage to Canterbury, has been read as an anagogical figure of a penitential journey. The pilgrims, "wayfarers to eternity," are making their way from Babylon, or Southwark, to the heavenly Jerusalem, or Canterbury. The Parson appears last among the storytellers because, as a priest, he fittingly replaces the Host as the docent who will lead the others to beatitude.[30] Something of this same kind of approach has also been exploited in a study of *Piers Plowman*.[31]

A more restricted resort to Biblical commentary and Christian concepts in general is represented in a second group of critics. Even in Old English poems, including *Beowulf* and *Maldon*, one may find passages and words which suggest an acquaintance with such aspects of Christian thought. For example, Old English *modgeþanc*, which normally would mean "mind" or "thought," seems from its context to approximate the sense of Greek *logos* and thus to refer to the second person of the Trinity.[32] Again, certain individual images and personifications in *Piers Plowman*—in particular the walnut simile (B-text, XI) and the speech of the character named Book (B-text, XVIII)—have been convincingly shown to stem from patristic tradition.[33]

The more extreme allegorical critics, those who feel justified in working out systematic fourfold explications of secular literature, have for the past few years been under attack. They are accused of assuming an implausible degree of access to Biblical commentaries on the part both of writers and their audiences, of applying to literature a stricter kind of analysis than was ever used on Scripture itself, of utilizing a single narrow approach to the virtual exclusion of all others, and of simplistically holding that all serious literature of the Middle Ages was consciously intended to promote Christian charity.[34]

Yet, the real values inherent in the critic's use of Biblical lore are undeniable. When a Biblical allusion in literature is accompanied by some indication, direct or oblique, that a further association or meaning was in the writer's mind, it is obviously important to investigate the standard glosses, such as the famous *Glossa Ordinaria*.[35] It is further helpful to observe whether certain interpretations may be shown to have achieved wide currency by reason of their inclusion in encyclopedias, moral treatises, sermons, or other literary works.

The use of Biblical material in *Pearl* provides a satisfying illustration. An element of central importance in the poem is the Pearl-maiden's extended sermon on the Parable of the Vineyard (Matt. 20:1-16) in the course of which she gives emphasis to the Biblical identification of the penny paid each of the laborers with the gift of eternal life. But certain details, especially in the final stanza with its allusion to the Eucharist, strongly suggest that the poet had another association in mind. This further association appears in Biblical lore, specifically in a commentary on the fourth petition of the Pater Noster which equates our daily bread—that is, the Host of the Eucharist—with the penny of St. Matthew's parable. Moreover, this interpretation is set forth in one of the most popular of the moral treatises, the *Ayenbite of Inwyt* and in the several other vernacular versions of the same work. Widely known as it almost certainly was, the penny-Host association must have conferred a special significance on the final stanza for the original audiences. For the reference there to the Body of Christ shown to us every day in Mass would have served for them as a direct reminiscence of the penny in the *Pearl's* sermon and thus as the unifying concept and the crowning summation of the poet's central message.[36]

The several approaches to criticism treated here do not exhaust the possibilities. Nothing, for example, has been said about critics who look for historical persons or allusions to historical events in literature. The author of a study of *Sir Gawain and the Green Knight*, for example, argues that the *Gawain*-poet was probably a dependent in the household of Enguerrand de Coucy, the French Earl of Bedford who married a daughter of Edward III. Furthermore, the efforts of the English royal house to woo Enguerrand away from his French allegiance may have furnished the plot of the romance, and a complimentary version of Enguerrand's character may be traced in the presentation of Gawain.[37]

FURTHER READINGS

Atkins, J. W. H., *English Literary Criticism: The Medieval Phase,* New York: Peter Smith, Publisher, 1952.

Baldwin, Charles Sears, *Medieval Rhetoric and Poetic,* Gloucester, Mass.: Peter Smith, Publisher, 1959.

Bloomfield, Morton W., "Symbolism in Medieval Literature," *MP,* LVI (1958), 73-81.

Lubac, Henri de, *Exégèse Médiévale, Les Quatres Sens de l'Ecriture,* 2 vols., Paris: Aubier, 1959-1964.

Notes

Chapter I. Social and Religious Backgrounds:
Old English Period

1. Poetic translations of *Widsith* and of many of the other poems cited in this chapter are to be found in *An Anthology of Old English Poetry*, Charles W. Kennedy, tr., New York: Oxford University Press, 1960. Prose renderings are given in *Anglo-Saxon Poetry*, R. K. Gordon, tr., Everyman's Library, rev. ed., New York: E. P. Dutton & Co., 1954.

2. See the ninth-century annals in *The Peterborough Chronicle*, Harry A. Rositzke, tr., New York: Columbia University Press, 1951, pp. 59-73. Extracts from the *Chronicle* are included in *Select Translations from Old English Prose*, Albert S. Cook and Chauncey B. Tinker, eds., Boston, Mass.: Ginn and Co., 1908, pp. 66-76.

3. See Alfred's Preface to Gregory's *Pastoral Care* in Cook and Tinker, *Select Translations . . .*, *op. cit.*, pp. 100-04, especially p. 102.

4. *Ibid.*, p. 273.

5. *Ibid.*, p. 32.

6. Ll. 312-13. For a translation of the poem, see *An Anthology of Old English Poetry*, *op. cit.*, pp. 161-69.

7. L. 455. For a full translation, see *Beowulf, the Oldest English Epic*, Charles W. Kennedy, tr., New York: Oxford University Press, 1940.

8. Ll. 572-73.

9. See C. L. Wrenn's supplement to R. W. Chambers, *Beowulf, An Introduction to the Study of the Poem with a Dis-*

cussion of the Stories of Offa and Finn, 3rd ed., Cambridge, Eng.: University Press, 1959, pp. 508 ff.

10. See Josiah Cox Russell, *British Medieval Population*, Albuquerque: University of New Mexico, 1948, pp. 246 ff.; see also Russell's "The Clerical Population of Medieval England," *Traditio*, II (1944), 177-212.

11. *Beowulf*, Friedrich Klaeber, ed., 3rd ed., Boston, Mass.: D. C. Heath and Co., 1941, p. li.

12. See the various essays in *An Anthology of Beowulf Criticism*, Lewis E. Nicholson, ed., Notre Dame, Ind.: University of Notre Dame Press, 1963.

Chapter II. Social and Religious Backgrounds: Middle English Period

1. The dramatic interplay among the Pilgrims is treated in Robert M. Lumiansky, *Of Sondry Folk: The Dramatic Principle in the Canterbury Tales*, Austin: University of Texas Press, 1955.

2. Josiah Cox Russell, *British Medieval Population*, Albuquerque: University of New Mexico Press, 1948, pp. 214 ff.

3. *Ibid.*, pp. 282 ff.

4. See the study of the township of Hitchin by Frederick Seebohm, *The English Village Community*, 4th ed., Cambridge, Eng.: University Press, 1926.

5. H. S. Bennett, *Life on the English Manor: A Study of Peasant Conditions*, 1150-1400, Cambridge, Eng.: University Press, 1948, pp. 4-5.

6. See the study of Wigston Magna by W. G. Hoskins, *The Midland Peasant: The Economic and Social History of a Leicestershire Village*, London: The Macmillan Company, 1957.

7. Valuable accounts of conditions in medieval communities are to be found in Lucy Toulmin Smith's "Town Life," in *Mediaeval England*, H. W. C. Davis, ed., Oxford, Eng.: The Clarendon Press, 1924, pp. 281-318; and Sylvia L. Thrupp, *The Merchant Class of Medieval England*, 1300-1500, Ann Arbor: University of Michigan Press, 1962.

8. Thrupp, *The Merchant Class . . .* , *op. cit.*, p. 52.

9. An enlightening view of the educational level in the fifteenth century is provided in H. S. Bennett, *The Pastons and Their England: Studies in an Age of Transition*, Cambridge, Eng.: University Press, 1951.

10. Caxton's career as a publisher and, to a certain extent, as

a literary man is set forth in William Blades, *The Biography and Typography of William Caxton, England's First Printer*, London: Trübner, 1878. Also helpful in connection with the question of literacy and the availability of books are Margaret Deanesly, "Vernacular Books in the Fourteenth and Fifteenth Centuries," *Modern Language Review*, XV (1920), 349-58; and H. S. Bennett, "The Author and His Public in the Fourteenth and Fifteenth Centuries," *Essays and Studies by Members of the English Association*, XXIII (1938), 7-24.

11. J. M. Manly and Edith Rickert, *The Text of the Canterbury Tales*, 8 vols., Chicago, Ill.: University of Chicago Press, 1940, I, 604-05.

12. Josiah Cox Russell, "The Clerical Population of Medieval England," *Traditio*, II (1944), 177-212, especially pp. 178-79. See also John R. H. Moorman, *Church Life in England in the Thirteenth Century*, Cambridge, Eng.: University Press, 1955, pp. 256-61, and *passim*; and W. A. Pantin, *The English Church in the Fourteenth Century*, Cambridge, Eng.: University Press, 1955, pp. 9-29, and *passim*.

13. *A Relation, or Rather a True Account, of the Island of England*, Charlotte A. Sneyd, tr., The Camden Society, XXXVII (1847), 22.

14. See, for example, the *Constitutiones* (1237) of Alexander of Stavensby, Bishop of Coventry and Lichfield, in *Concilia Magnae Britanniae et Hiberniae*, David Wilkins, ed., London, 1737, I, 640-46. Especially helpful in explaining the effects of the new legislation is Moorman, *Church Life . . . op. cit.*, pp. 90 ff.

15. Cited in J. W. Adamson, "The Extent of Literacy in England in the Fifteenth and Sixteenth Centuries: Notes and Conjectures," *The Library*, 4th Ser., X (1929), 183.

16. Printed in Wilkins, *Concilia Magnae . . . op. cit.*, II, 51 ff., especially p. 54.

17. *Liber Tercius*, in *The Complete Works of John Gower*, G. C. Macaulay, ed., Oxford, Eng.: The Clarendon Press, 1899-1902, IV, 105 ff. This entire book is given over to a criticism of the Church, including the prelacy, priesthood, and regular clergy. In his lengthy English work, *Confessio Amantis*, Gower includes a briefer attack on the Church, *Prologus*, 11. 193-498 (*ed. cit.*, II, 11-18). A translation of *Vox Clamantis* is to be found in *The Major Latin Works of John Gower*, Eric W. Stockton, tr., Seattle: University of Washington Press, 1962.

18. Moorman, *Church Life* . . . , *op. cit.*, *passim;* and Pantin, *The English Church* . . . , *op. cit.*, pp. 9-29, and *passim.* Both cite instances of clerical shortcomings.

19. *Life on the English Manor*, pp. 326 ff.

20. *Mirk's Festial: A Collection of Homilies Edited from Bodl. MS. Gough Eccl. Top. 4*, Theodor Erb, ed., Early English Text Society, Extra Series, XCVI (1905), 171.

21. Frederick J. Furnivall, ed., Early English Text Society, CXIX, CXXIII (1901, 1903), ll. 4260-61.

22. The text of this decree of the Fourth Lateran Council is printed in Henry Denzinger, *Enchiridion Symbolorum*, Carolus Rahner, ed., Freiburg, Germany: Herder, 1953, pp. 204-05.

Chapter III. The English Language in the Middle Ages

1. *The Poems of John Dryden*, John Sargeaunt, ed., London: Oxford University Press, 1929, p. 276.

2. *The Works of Geoffrey Chaucer*, F. N. Robinson, ed., 2nd ed., Boston, Mass.: Houghton Mifflin Company, 1957, p. 84, ll. 882-83.

3. *Ed. cit.*, p. 335, ll. 46-48.

4. *þe Desputisoun bitwen þe Bodi and þe Soule*, Wilhelm Linow, ed., *Erlanger Beiträge zur englischen Philologie*, I (1889), ll. 1-4. The symbol ʒ appearing in several words of this passage and also in other poetry and prose cited in this chapter has the phonetic value of *ch* in German *ich*. They symbol þ is equivalent to Modern English *th*.

5. In Linow, *op. cit.*, Anhang II, p. 200, ll. 1-5.

6. *The Translations of Ezra Pound*, Hugh Kenner, ed., London: Faber and Faber, 1953.

7. A short list of recordings is appended to the Further Readings at the end of Chapter III. One view of the way in which the *scop* used his harp is set forth by Robert Creed in *Beowulf*, Burton Raffel, tr., New York: Mentor Books, New American Library, 1963, pp. 133-37.

8. *Beowulf*, Friedrich Klaeber, ed., 3rd ed., Boston, Mass.: D. C. Heath and Co., 1950, ll. 2801-08.

9. Very instructive in this connection is C. S. Lewis's poem "The Planets," written in conformity with Old English poetic principles, in *Rehabilitations and Other Essays*, London: Oxford University Press, 1939, pp. 129-32.

10. Francis B. Gummere, *The Oldest English Epic*, New York: The Macmillan Company, 1927, ll. 2801-08.

11. *Beowulf, the Oldest English Epic*, Charles W. Kennedy, tr., New York: Oxford University Press, 1940, ll. 2801-08.

12. In *Bright's Anglo-Saxon Reader*, rev. ed., James R. Hulbert, New York: Henry Holt, 1945, p. 84.

13. *Two of the Saxon Chronicles Parallel*, Charles Plummer and John Earle, eds., 2 vols., Oxford, Eng.: The Clarendon Press, 1892, I, 91.

14. *Ibid.*, I, 219.

15. In *Pearl and Sir Gawain and the Green Knight*, A. C. Cawley, ed., Everyman's Library, London: J. M. Dent & Sons, 1962, l. 1065. The texts in this edition are somewhat modernized.

16. *Love's Labours Lost*, II, i, 184-85.

17. *One Hundred Middle English Lyrics*, Robert D. Stevick, ed., Indianapolis, Ind.: Bobbs-Merrill Company, 1964.

18. Layamon (or Lawman), *Brut*, in Fernand Mossé, *A Handbook of Middle English*, James A. Walker, tr., Baltimore, Md.: The Johns Hopkins Press, 1952, p. 153, ll. 16-22. For a translation of the *Brut* of both Layamon and Wace, see *Arthurian Chronicles*, Everyman's Library, London: J. M. Dent & Sons, 1937.

19. Eric Gerald Stanley, ed., London: Thomas Nelson and Sons, 1960, ll. 1-4. For a modern verse rendering, see *The Owl and the Nightingale*, Graydon Eggers, tr., Durham, N. C.: Duke University Press, 1955.

20. In Mossé, *op. cit.*, p. 201, ll. 3–7.

21. In *Pearl and Sir Gawain and the Green Knight, ed. cit.*, p. 51, ll. 1-7.

22. *Ancrene Riwle* (or *Ancrene Wisse*), in Mossé, *op. cit.*, p. 147, ll. 123-25. For a translation, see *The Ancrene Riwle*, M. B. Salu, tr., London: Burns, Oates, 1955.

23. *The Love of God*, in Mossé, *op. cit.*, p. 233, ll. 88-91.

24. *The Tale of Melibee*, in *The Works of Geoffrey Chaucer, ed. cit.*, p. 167.

25. *The Works of Sir Thomas Malory*, 1 vol. ed., Eugène Vinaver, ed., London: Oxford University Press, 1964, pp. 870-71.

Chapter IV. Popular Christian Doctrine

1. Ronald S. Crane, "Literature, Philosophy, and the History of Ideas," MP, LII (1954), 73-83.

2. *The Works of Geoffrey Chaucer, ed. cit.*, p. 203, ll. 3240-45.

3. *The Discarded Image, An Introduction to Medieval and*

Renaissance Literature, Cambridge, Eng.: University Press, 1964, p. 75. Boethius, *The Consolation of Philosophy*, tr. and rev. by H. F. Stewart, Loeb Classical Library, Cambridge, Mass.: Harvard University Press, 1953. A convenient abridgment, including a commentary by Whitney J. Oates, is *Boethius, The Consolation of Philosophy*, James J. Buchanan, tr., New York: Frederick Ungar Publishing Company, 1957.

4. Translated passages from this and from other important philosophical and theological works referred to in this chapter may be found in *Selections from Medieval Philosophers*, Richard McKeon, ed. and tr., 2 vols., New York: Charles Scribner's Sons, 1929, 1930.

5. See *Basic Writings of Saint Thomas Aquinas*, Anton C. Pegis, ed., New York: Random House, 1945.

6. John Jay Parry, tr., New York: Columbia University Press, 1941. A convenient abridgment, including a summary, is *Andreas Capellanus, The Art of Courtly Love*, Frederick W. Locke, ed., New York: Frederick Ungar Publishing Company, 1957.

7. *Ed. cit.*, p. 150, ll. 538-40.

8. *Ibid.*, p. 46, ll. 2987-93.

9. Evelyn Underhill, *The Essentials of Mysticism and Other Essays*, London: J. M. Dent & Sons, 1920; and Conrad Pepler, *The English Religious Heritage*, St. Louis, Mo.: B. Herder Book Co., 1958.

10. See Robert Steele, *Mediaeval Lore from Bartholomeus Anglicus*, London: Chatto and Windus, 1924.

11. See the selections from the Old English *Physiologus* in *Anglo-Saxon Poetry*, R. K. Gordon, tr., Everyman, rev. ed., London, J. M. Dent & Sons, 1954, pp. 252-55. The text and translation are available in *The Old English Physiologus*, Albert S. Cook and James Hall Pitman, eds. and trs., Yale Studies in English, LXIII (1921).

12. This classification of religious treatises is taken from W. A. Pantin, *The English Church in the Fourteenth Century*, Cambridge, Eng.: University Press, 1955, pp. 189-223.

13. *Orologium Sapientiae, or The Seven Poyntes of Trewe Wisdom*, K. Horstmann, ed., *Anglia*, X (1888), 328.

14. *Instructions for Parish Priests by John Myrc*, Edward Peacock, ed., Early English Text Society, XXXI (1868), 13, ll. 422-25.

15. *Ibid.*, p. 14, ll. 426-37.

16. *Lay Folks Catechism, or the English and Latin Version of Archbishop Thoresby's Instruction for the People,* Thomas Frederick Simmons and Henry Edward Nolloth, eds., Early English Text Society, CXVIII (1901), 22-30, ll. 77-161.

17. *Ibid.,* pp. 20-81, ll. 51 ff. The discussion of the senses appears on pp. 18-19, ll. 330-58.

18. *Dan Michel's Ayenbite of Inwyt, or Remorse of Conscience,* Richard Morris, ed., Early English Text Society, XXIII (1866), 14 ff. For a partial translation, see *The Ayenbite of Inwyt,* A. J. Wyatt, tr., London: W. B. Clive and Co., n.d.

19. Arthur Brandeis, ed., Early English Text Society, CXV (1900), 1-5.

20. *Le Livre de Seyntz Medicines,* E. J. Arnould, ed., Anglo-Norman Texts, II (1940).

21. *The Desert of Religion,* Walter Hübner, ed., *Archiv für das Studium der neueren Sprachen und Literaturen,* CXXVI (1911), 58-74.

22. For discussions and some reproductions of religious diagrams, wall paintings, and other kinds of ecclesiastical art, see Mary Desirée Anderson, *Drama and Imagery in English Medieval Churches,* Cambridge, Eng.: University Press, 1963; and E. W. Tristram, *English Wall-Painting of the Fourteenth Century,* London: Routledge and Kegan Paul, 1955.

23. *The Poems of William of Shoreham,* M. Konrath, ed., Early English Text Society, Extra Series, LXXXVI (1902).

24. *The Prymer, or Lay Folk's Prayer Book,* Henry Littlehales, ed., Early English Text Society, CV, CIX (1895, 1897).

25. John Lydgate, *Merita Missae,* in *The Lay Folks Mass-Book,* Thomas Frederick Simmons, ed., Early English Text Society, LXXI (1879), 148-54.

26. *Mirk's Festial: A Collection of Homilies Edited from Bodl. MS. Gough Eccl. Top. 4,* Theodor Erbe, ed., Early English Text Society, Extra Series, XCVI (1905), 168-71.

27. *The Pricke of Conscience,* Richard Morris, ed., *The Philological Society,* London, 1863, ll. 3762 ff.

28. For discussions of medieval knowledge of the Bible, see Beryl Smalley, *The Study of the Bible in the Middle Ages,* Oxford, Eng.: Basil Blackwell, 1952; and H. H. Glunz, *History of the Vulgate in England from Alcuin to Roger Bacon,* Cambridge, Eng.: University Press, 1933.

29. *Mirk's Festial, ed. cit.,* pp. 101-03.

30. *Cursor Mundi*, Richard Morris, ed., Early English Text Society, LVII, LIX, LXII, LXVI, LXVIII, XCIX, CI (1874-1893).

Chapter V. The World View of the Middle Ages

1. *Byrhtferth's Manual*, S. J. Crawford, ed., Early English Text Society, CLXXVII (1929).

2. C. S. Lewis, *The Discarded Image, An Introduction to Medieval and Renaissance Literature*, Cambridge, Eng.: University Press, 1964, p. 20.

3. See Lewis, *op. cit.*; and also A. O. Lovejoy, *The Great Chain of Being: A Study in the History of an Idea*, Cambridge, Mass.: Harvard University Press, 1936.

4. *The Works of Geoffrey Chaucer*, F. N. Robinson, ed., 2nd ed., Boston: Houghton Mifflin Company, 1957, p. 545.

5. *The Equatorie of the Planetis*, Derek J. Price, ed., Cambridge, Eng.: University Press, 1955.

6. See Galileo Galilei, *Dialogue on the Great World Systems, in the Salisbury Translation*, rev. and ed. by Giorgio Santillana, Chicago, Ill.: University of Chicago Press, 1953, pp. 335 ff.; and also in the same work the "Historical Introduction," pp. xi-li, and "An Astronomical Note on the Two Systems," pp. 475-96.

7. *The South English Legendary*, Charlotte D'Evelyn and Anna J. Mill, eds., Early English Text Society, CCXXXV, CCXXXVI, CCXLV (1956-1959), 402-28.

8. Robert Steele, *Mediaeval Lore from Bartholomeus Anglicus*, London: Chatto and Windus, 1924, pp. 28-30.

9. *Caxton's Mirrour of the World*, Oliver H. Prior, ed., Early English Text Society, Extra Series, CX (1913), 68 ff.

10. John Lydgate, *The Pilgrimage of the Life of Man Englisht by John Lydgate*, F. J. Furnivall, ed., Early English Text Society, Extra Series, LXXVII, LXXXIII, XCII (1899-1904), ll. 20611-22.

11. *The Pricke of Conscience*, Richard Morris, ed., *The Philological Society*, London, 1863, ll. 1042 ff.

12. *The Poems of William of Shoreham*, M. Konrath, ed., Early English Text Society, Extra Series, LXXXVI (1902), 131-132, ll. 43-78.

13. *Ed. cit.*, pp. 451-52, Book IV, ll. 958-1082. See the discussion of this passage in Sanford B. Meech, *Design in Chaucer's Troilus*, Syracuse, N. Y.: Syracuse University Press, 1959, *passim*.

14. Walter Clyde Curry, "Destiny in Chaucer's *Troilus*," *PMLA*, XLV (1930), 129-68.

15. *Clerk's Tale, The*, in *The Works of Geoffrey Chaucer*, ed. *cit.*, p. 114, ll. 1152-62.

16. See Theodore Otto Wedel, *The Mediæval Attitude Toward Astrology Particularly in England*, Yale Studies in English, LX (1920), 4-8, and *passim*.

17. *General Prologue*, in *The Works of Geoffrey Chaucer*, ed. *cit.*, p. 21, ll. 411-21.

18. See Curry, *op. cit.*; and Wedel, *op. cit.*, pp. 9 ff.

Appendix: Critical Approaches

1. *Les arts poétiques du XIIe et XIIIe siècle*, Edmond Faral, ed., Paris: Librairie Honoré Champion, 1958.

2. *The Proceedings of the British Academy*, XII (1926), 95-113.

3. See, for example, George J. Engelhardt, "*Beowulf*: A Study in Dilatation," *PMLA*, LXX (1955), 825-52.

4. See, for example, Marie P. Hamilton, "Notes on Chaucer and the Rhetoricians," *PMLA*, XLVII (1932), 403-09; and Helge Kökeritz, "Rhetorical Word-Play in Chaucer," *PMLA*, LXIX (1954), 937-52.

5. See A. C. Spearing, *Criticism and Medieval Poetry*, New York: Barnes & Noble, 1964, pp. 66 ff.

6. *Nun's Priest's Tale, The*, in *The Works of Geoffrey Chaucer*, F. N. Robinson, ed., 2nd ed., Boston, Mass.: Houghton Mifflin Company, 1957, p. 204, l. 3347.

7. James J. Murphy, "A New Look at Chaucer and the Rhetoricians," *RES*, XV (1964), 1-20; and the same author's "Rhetoric in Fourteenth-Century Oxford," *MAE*, XXXIV (1965), 1-20.

8. Spearing, *op. cit.*, p. 61, and *passim*.

9. See Helen Gardner, *The Limits of Criticism*, London: Oxford University Press, 1956.

10. P. Steinbach, cited in Robert W. Ackerman, "English Rimed and Prose Romances," in *Arthurian Literature in the Middle Ages*, Roger S. Loomis, ed., Oxford, Eng.: The Clarendon Press, 1959, pp. 507 ff. The standard edition of this romance is *Ywain and Gawain*, Albert B. Friedman and Norman T. Harrington, eds., Early English Text Society, CCLIV (1964).

11. Meech, *Design in Chaucer's Troilus*, Syracuse, N.Y.: Syracuse University Press, 1959.

12. R. M. Lumiansky, *Malory's Originality: A Critical Study of Le Morte Darthur*, Baltimore, Md.: The Johns Hopkins Press, 1964; and Charles Moorman, *The Book of King Arthur: The Unity of Malory's Morte Darthur*, Lexington: University of Kentucky Press, 1965.

13. *The Works of Sir Thomas Malory*, Eugène Vinaver, ed., Oxford, Eng.: The Clarendon Press, 1947, I, lvii, etc. Also on this subject, see *Essays on Malory*, J. A. W. Bennett, ed., Oxford, Eng.: The Clarendon Press, 1963.

14. Roger Sherman Loomis, *The Grail from Celtic Myth to Christian Symbol*, New York: Columbia University Press, 1963.

15. K. Müllenhoff's essay on the "inner history of Beowulf" is particularly interesting in this connection. See the review of scholarship in *Beowulf*, Friedrich Klaeber, ed., 3rd ed., Boston, Mass.: D. C. Heath and Co., 1941, pp. cii ff.

16. See various numbers of the *FF* [Folklore Fellows] *Communications*, published in Helsinki.

17. For a general discussion of folklore, see Stith Thompson, *The Folktale*, New York: Dryden Press, 1946; and Francis Lee Utley, "Folklore, Myth, and Ritual," in *Critical Approaches to Medieval Literature*, Selected English Institute Papers, 1958-1959, Dorothy Bethurum, ed., New York: Columbia University Press, 1960, pp. 83-109.

18. See *Beowulf, ed. cit.*, pp. xxiii ff.; and W. W. Lawrence, *Beowulf and Epic Tradition*, Cambridge, Mass.: Harvard University Press, 1928.

19. Otto Rank, "Der Sinn der Griselda-Fabel," *Imago*, I (1912), 34-48.

20. Jessie L. Weston, *From Ritual to Romance*, Cambridge, Mass.: Harvard University Press, 1920.

21. John Speirs, *Medieval English Poetry: The Non-Chaucerian Tradition*, New York: The Macmillan Company, 1958, especially pp. 210 ff.

22. See *Rhetorica ad Herennium*, ed. and tr. by Harry Caplan, Loeb Classical Library, Cambridge, Mass.: Harvard University Press, 1954.

23. See Helen Flanders Dunbar, *Symbolism in Medieval Thought and Its Consummation in the Divine Comedy*, New Haven, Conn.: Yale University Press, 1929.

24. See, for example, Etienne Gilson, *Dante the Philosopher*, David Moore, tr., New York: Sheed and Ward, 1949; and Charles

S. Singleton, "Dante's Allegory," *Speculum*, XXV (1950), 78-86.

25. D. W. Robertson, Jr., "The Pearl as a Symbol," *MLN*, LXV (1950), 155-57.

26. Hans Schnyder, *Sir Gawain and the Green Knight: An Essay in Interpretation*, Cooper Monographs, 6, Berne: Francke, 1961.

27. Charles A. Owen, Jr., "The Crucial Passages in Five of the *Canterbury Tales*: A Study in Irony and Symbol," *JEGP*, LII (1953), 294-311.

28. Robert P. Miller, "Chaucer's Pardoner, the Scriptural Eunuch, and *The Pardoner's Tale*," *Speculum*, XXX (1955), 180-99.

29. Owen, *op. cit.*

30. Ralph Baldwin, "The Unity of *The Canterbury Tales*," *Anglistica*, V (1965).

31. D. W. Robertson, Jr., and Bernard F. Huppé, *Piers Plowman and Scriptural Tradition*, Princeton, N. J.: Princeton University Press, 1951.

32. Morton W. Bloomfield, "Patristics and Old English Literature: Notes on some Poems," *CL*, XIV (1962), 36-43.

33. R. E. Kaske, "Langland's Walnut Simile," *JEGP*, LVIII (1959), 650-54; and the same author's "The Speech of 'Book' in *Piers Plowman*," *Anglia*, LXVII (1959), 117-44.

34. R. S. Crane, "On Hypotheses in Literary Interpretation Apropos of Certain Medievalists," unpublished paper read before the Modern Language Association of America, December, 1961; Charles Donahue, "Patristic Exegesis in the Criticism of Medieval Literature: Summation," pp. 61-82, E. Talbot Donaldson, "Patristic Exegesis in the Criticism of Medieval Literature: The Opposition," pp. 1-26, and R. E. Kaske, "Patristic Exegesis in the Criticism of Medieval Literature: The Defense," pp. 27-60, all in *Critical Approaches to Medieval Literature*, Dorothy Bethurum, ed., *op. cit.*

35. *Glossa Ordinaria, Walafridi Strabi Fuldensis Monachi Opera Omnia*, in *Patrologia Latina*, J. P. Migne, ed., CXIII, CXIV (1879). On the *Glossa Ordinaria*, see H. H. Glunz, *History of the Vulgate in England from Alcuin to Roger Bacon*, Cambridge, Eng.: University Press, 1933; and Beryl Smalley, *The Study of the Bible in the Middle Ages*, 2nd ed., Oxford, Eng.: Basil Blackwell, 1952.

It should be noted that the *Glossa Ordinaria* provides a commentary on a high proportion but by no means on all the verses in the Vulgate Bible. The authors of the glosses are identified as Origen, Augustine, Chrysostom, Jerome, Ambrose, Gregory, Rabanus Maurus, Bede, Alcuin, and the like, the works of Augustine being most frequently cited. One should not expect that every verse receiving attention is glossed on all the four levels of interpretation. Most of the commentaries, in fact, dwell on only one level of the figurative meaning of a word, name, phrase, or verse. That is, not everything in the Bible yields a full set of spiritual meanings.

Very likely, most literate persons, including the clergy, gained a knowledge of only those individual interpretations which were taken up by the encyclopedists and other popularizers. In general, Biblical commentary was the province of the scholars and theologians.

36. Robert W. Ackerman, "The Pearl-Maiden and the Penny," *RPh*, XVII (1964), 615-24.

37. Henry L. Savage, *The Gawain-Poet: Studies in His Personality and Background*, Chapel Hill: University of North Carolina Press, 1956.

Selective

Bibliography

A. MEDIEVAL TEXTS

Listed below are the principal works **quoted** *or referred to throughout the book, whether Old English, Middle English, Latin, or Anglo-Norman. Standard critical editions are normally given here even though, as indicated in the footnotes, the passages quoted in the foregoing pages tend to be taken from anthologies or translations more readily accessible to the student.*

Ælfric, *The Homilies of the Anglo-Saxon Church*, B. Thorpe, ed., 2 vols., London: The Ælfric Society, 1844-1846.

Alfred, King, *King Alfred's Old English Version of Boethius' De Consolatione Philosophiae*, Walter John Sedgefield, ed., Oxford, Eng.: The Clarendon Press, 1899.

——, *King Alfred's West-Saxon Version of Gregory's Pastoral Care*, Henry Sweet, ed., Early English Text Society, XLV, L (1871; reprinted 1930 and 1934).

Ancrene Riwle (or *Ancrene Wisse*), various English texts, Albert C. Baugh, ed., Early English Text Society, CCXXXII (1956); Mabel Day, ed., Early English Text Society, CCXXV (1952); and Richard M. Wilson, ed., Early English Text Society, CCXXIX (1954).

Andreas Capellanus, *The Art of Courtly Love*, John Jay Parry, tr., New York: Columbia University Press, 1941.

Ayenbite of Inwyt, Dan Michel's Ayenbite of Inwyt, or Remorse of Conscience, Richard Morris, ed., Early English Text Society, XXIII (1866).

Bede, *Ecclesiastical History of the English Nation*, in *Bœdae*

Opera Historica, J. E. King, ed., 2 vols., Loeb Classical Library, London: Wm. Heinemann, 1930.

Beowulf, and the Fight at Finnsburg, Friedrich Klaeber, ed., 3rd ed., Boston, Mass.: D. C. Heath and Co., 1941.

Boethius, *The Consolation of Philosophy*, tr. and rev. by H. F. Stewart and E. K. Rand, Loeb Classical Library, Cambridge, Mass.: Harvard University Press, 1953.

Brinton, Thomas, *The Sermons of Thomas Brinton, Bishop of Rochester* (1373-1389), Sister Mary Aquinas Devlin, ed., The Camden Society, 3rd Ser., LXXXV, LXXXVI (1954).

Brunanburh, in *The Anglo-Saxon Minor Poems*, E. V. K. Dobbie, ed., "The Anglo-Saxon Poetic Records," Vol. VI, New York: Columbia University Press, 1942.

Byrhtferth's Manual, S. J. Crawford, ed., Early English Text Society, CLXXVII (1929).

Cædmon, in *The Junius Manuscript*, George Philip Krapp, ed., "The Anglo-Saxon Poetic Records," Vol. I, New York: Columbia University Press, 1931.

Caxton, William, see *Mirrour of the World*.

Charms, see *Leechdoms*.

Chaucer, Geoffrey, *The Works of*, F. N. Robinson, ed., 2nd ed., Boston, Mass.: Houghton Mifflin Company, 1957.

Christ, in *The Exeter Book*, George Philip Krapp and E. V. K. Dobbie, eds., "The Anglo-Saxon Poetic Records," Vol. III, New York: Columbia University Press, 1936.

Corpus Glossary, The, W. M. Lindsay, ed., Cambridge, Eng.: University Press, 1921.

Cursor Mundi, Richard Morris, ed., Early English Text Society, LVII, LIX, LXII, LXVI, LXVIII, XCIX, CI (1874-1893).

Debate of the Body and the Soul, The, þe Desputisoun bitwen þe Bodi and þe Soule, Wilhelm Linow, ed., *Erlanger Beiträge zur englischen Philologie*, I (1889).

Deonise Hid Diuinite, Phyllis Hodgson, ed., Early English Text Society, CCXXXI (1955).

Deor, in *The Exeter Book*, George Philip Krapp and E. V. K. Dobbie, eds., "The Anglo-Saxon Poetic Records," Vol. III, New York: Columbia University Press, 1936.

Desert of Religion, The, Walter Hübner, ed., *Archiv für das Studium der neueren Sprachen und Literaturen*, CXXVI (1911), 58-74.

Dream of the Rood, The, in *The Vercelli Book*, George Philip

Krapp, ed., "The Anglo-Saxon Poetic Records," Vol. II, New York: Columbia University Press, 1932.

Edmund, St., *The Mirror of St. Edmund* in *Religious Pieces in Prose and Verse*, George G. Perry, ed., Early English Text Society, XXVI (1867).

Elene, in *The Vercelli Book*, George Philip Krapp, ed., "The Anglo-Saxon Poetic Records," Vol. II, New York: Columbia University Press, 1932.

Equatorie of the Planetis, The, Derek Price, ed., Cambridge, Eng.: University Press, 1955.

Finnsburg, in *The Anglo-Saxon Minor Poems*, E. V. K. Dobbie, ed., "The Anglo-Saxon Poetic Records," Vol. VI, New York: Columbia University Press, 1942.

Gawain and the Green Knight, Sir, Sir Israel Gollancz, ed., Early English Text Society, CCX (1940).

Gildas, The Works of, in *Six Old English Chronicles*, J. A. Giles, tr., London: Bell, 1885.

Gower, John, The Complete Works of, G. C. Macaulay, ed., 4 vols., Oxford, Eng.: The Clarendon Press, 1899-1902.

Henry of Lancaster, *Livre de Seyntz Medicines*, E. J. Arnould, ed., Anglo-Norman Texts, II (1940).

Hilton, Walter, *The Ladder of Perfection*, Leo Sherley-Price, tr., Penguin Books, 1957.

Jacob's Well, Arthur Brandeis, ed., Early English Text Society, CXV (1900).

Julian of Norwich, *Revelations of Divine Love Shewed to a Devout Ankress*, Dom Roger Hudleston, ed., 2nd ed., London: Burns, Oates, 1952.

Juliana, in *The Exeter Book*, George Philip Krapp and E. V. K. Dobbie, eds., "The Anglo-Saxon Poetic Records," Vol. III, New York: Columbia University Press, 1936.

Layamon, *Brut*, G. L. Brook and R. F. Leslie, eds., Vol. I, Early English Text Society, CCL (1963).

Lay Folk's Massbook, The, Thomas Frederick Simmons, ed., Early English Text Society, LXXI (1879).

Leechdoms, in *Leechdoms, Wortcunning and Starcraft of Early England*, Thomas O. Cockayne, ed., 3 vols., London: Longmans, 1864-1866.

Lovelich, Henry, *The Holy Grail*, Frederick J. Furnivall, ed., Early English Text Society, Extra Series, XX, XXIV, XXV-III, XXX, XCV (1874-1905).

———, *Merlin*, Ernst A. Koch, ed., Early English Text Society,

Extra Series, XCIII (1904), CXII (1913), and Original Series, CLXXXV (1932).

Lucretius, *De Rerum Natura*, R. C. Trevelyan, tr., Cambridge, Eng.: University Press, 1937.

Lydgate, John, *The Pilgrimage of the Life of Man Englisht by John Lydgate*, F. J. Furnivall, ed., Early English Text Society, Extra Series, LXXVII, LXXXIII, XCII (1899-1904).

Maldon, in *The Anglo-Saxon Minor Poems*, E. V. K. Dobbie, ed., "The Anglo-Saxon Poetic Records," Vol. VI, New York: Columbia University Press, 1942.

Malory, Sir Thomas, *The Works of Sir Thomas Malory*, Eugène Vinaver, ed., 3 vols., Oxford, Eng.: The Clarendon Press, 1947.

Mannyng, Robert, of Brunne, *Handlyng Synne*, Frederick J. Furnivall, ed., Early English Text Society, CXIX, CXXIII (1901-1903).

Mirrour of the World, [*Caxton's*], Oliver H. Prior, ed., Early English Text Society, Extra Series, CX (1913).

Moral Ode (or *Poema Morale*), in *Das frühmittelenglische "Poema Morale" kritisch herausgegeben*, H. Marcus, ed., *Palaestra*, CXCIV (1934).

Morte Arthure (alliterative *Morte Arthure*), Erik Björkman, ed., *Alt- und Mittelenglische Texte*, IX (1915).

Myrc, John, *Instructions for Parish Priests by John Myrc*, Edward Peacock, ed., Early English Text Society, XXXI (1868).

————, *Mirk's Festial: A Collection of Homilies Edited from Bodl. MS. Gough Eccl. Top. 4*, Theodor Erbe, ed., Early English Text Society, XCVI (1905).

Neckam, Alexander, *De Naturis Rerum*, Thomas Wright, ed., *Chronicles and Memorials of Great Britain and Ireland During the Middle Ages*, London: Longmans, Green, 1863.

Orologium Sapientiae, or The Seven Poyntes of Trewe Wisdom, K. Horstmann, ed., *Anglia*, X (1888).

Owl and the Nightingale, The, Eric Gerald Stanley, ed., London: Thomas Nelson and Sons, 1960.

Pearl, E. V. Gordon, ed., Oxford, Eng.: The Clarendon Press, 1953.

Physiologus, The Old English, ed. and tr. by Albert S. Cook and James Hall Pitman, Yale Studies in English, LXIII (1921).

Piers Plowman, The Vision of, W. W. Skeat, ed., 2 vols., London: Oxford University Press, 1924.

Pricke of Conscience, The, Richard Morris, ed., The Philological Society (1863).

Prymer, or Lay Folk's Prayer Book, The, Henry Littlehales, ed., Early English Text Society, CV, CIX (1895-1897).

Rolle, Richard, *The English Writings of Richard Rolle,* Hope Emily Allen, ed., Oxford, Eng.: The Clarendon Press, 1931.

Ruin, The, in *The Exeter Book,* George Philip Krapp and E. V. K. Dobbie, eds., "The Anglo-Saxon Poetic Records," Vol. III, New York: Columbia University Press, 1936.

Saxon Chronicle (or *Anglo-Saxon Chronicle*), John Earle and Charles Plummer, eds., 2 vols., Oxford, Eng.: The Clarendon Press, 1892.

Seafarer, The, in *The Exeter Book,* George Philip Krapp and E. V. K. Dobbie, eds., "The Anglo-Saxon Poetic Records," Vol. III, New York: Columbia University Press, 1936.

South English Legendary, The, Charlotte D'Evelyn and Anna J. Mill, eds., Early English Text Society, CCXXXV, CCXXXVI, CCXLIV (1956-1959).

Thoresby, John, *Lay Folk's Catechism, or The English and Latin Version of Archbishop Thoresby's Instruction for the People;* Thomas Frederick Simmons and Henry Edward Nolloth, eds., Early English Text Society, CXVIII (1901).

Vices and Virtues, The Book of, W. Nelson Francis, ed., Early English Text Society, CCXVII (1942).

Waldere, in *The Anglo-Saxon Minor Poems,* E. V. K. Dobbie, ed., "The Anglo-Saxon Poetic Records," Vol. VI, New York: Columbia University Press, 1942.

Wanderer, The, in *The Exeter Book,* George Philip Krapp and E. V. K. Dobbie, eds., "The Anglo-Saxon Poetic Records," Vol. III, New York: Columbia University Press, 1936.

Widsith, in *The Exeter Book,* George Philip Krapp and E. V. K. Dobbie, eds., "The Anglo-Saxon Poetic Records," Vol. III, New York: Columbia University Press, 1936.

William of Shoreham, The Poems of, M. Konrath, ed., Early English Text Society, Extra Series, LXXXVI (1902).

Wulfstan, *Sermo Lupi ad Anglos,* Dorothy Whitelock, ed., 2nd ed., London: Methuen, 1952.

Ywain and Gawain, Albert B. Friedman and Norman T. Harrington, eds., Early English Text Society, CCLIV (1964).

B. OTHER WORKS CONSULTED

The following books and articles are intended as a supplement to the citations in the footnotes and the Further Readings at the end of each chapter.

Bliss, A. J., "The Appreciation of Old English Metre," in *English and Medieval Studies Presented to J. R. R. Tolkien on the Occasion of His Seventieth Birthday*, Norman Davis and C. L. Wrenn, eds., London: George Allen & Unwin, 1962.

Brodeur, Arthur G., *The Art of Beowulf*, Berkeley: University of California Press, 1959.

Chambers, John David, *Divine Worship in England in the Thirteenth and Fourteenth Centuries*, London: Pickering, 1877.

Deanesly, Margaret, *A History of the Medieval Church, 590-1500*, London: Methuen, 1925.

Haber, T. B., *A Comparative Study of the Beowulf and the Aeneid*, Princeton, N. J.: Princeton University Press, 1931.

Hodgkin, R. H., *A History of the Anglo-Saxons*, 3rd ed., 2 vols., London: Oxford University Press, 1952.

Hulbert, James R., "The Genesis of Beowulf: A Caveat," PMLA, LXVI (1951), 1168-76.

Knowles, Dom David, *The Religious Orders in England*, 2 vols., Cambridge, Eng.: University Press, 1956, 1957.

Legge, M. Dominica, *Anglo-Norman Literature and its Background*, Oxford, Eng.: The Clarendon Press, 1963.

McKisack, May, *The Fourteenth Century, 1307-1399*, Oxford, Eng.: The Clarendon Press, 1959.

Magoun, Francis P., Jr., "Oral-Formulaic Character of Anglo-Saxon Narrative Poetry," *Speculum*, XXVIII (1953), 446-67.

Makarewicz, Sister Mary, *The Patristic Influence on Chaucer*, Washington, D.C.: Catholic University of America Press, 1953.

Pope, John Collins, *The Rhythm of Beowulf*, New Haven, Conn.: Yale University Press, 1942.

Powicke, Sir Maurice, *The Thirteenth Century, 1216-1307*, Oxford, Eng.: The Clarendon Press, 1954.

Previté-Orton, C. W., *The Shorter Cambridge Medieval History*, 2 vols., Cambridge, Eng.: University Press, 1953.

Rashdall, Hastings, *The Universities of Europe in the Middle Ages*, F. N. Powicke and A. B. Emden, eds., 3 vols., Oxford, Eng.: The Clarendon Press, 1936.

Robertson, D. W., Jr., "The Doctrine of Charity in Medieval

Literary Gardens: A Topical Approach Through Symbolism and Allegory," *Speculum*, XXVI (1951), 24-49.

Rogers, James E. Thorold, *Six Centuries of Work and Wages: The History of English Labour*, 2 vols., New York: G. P. Putnam's Sons, n.d.

Trevelyan, G. M., *Illustrated English Social History*, Vol. I, *Chaucer's England and the Early Tudors*, London: Longmans, Green, 1942.

Underhill, Evelyn, *Mysticism*, 12th ed., rev., London: Methuen, 1930.

Index